THE LITTLE BOOK OF
FOOTBALL

Written by Michael Heatley

THE LITTLE BOOK OF
FOOTBALL

First published in the UK in 2007

© G2 Entertainment Limited 2013

www.G2ent.co.uk

Printed and bound in China

ISBN 978-1-782812-05-0

Contents

Chapter 1

Origins of the Game

IT IS NOW WELL OVER A CENTURY since association football – also commonly known as soccer, to differentiate it first from rugby football, then American football – was first played in an organised fashion, much longer since the Romans played a ball-based contact sport. Yet here in the twenty-first century the game retains its position as the most popular in the world.

Its appeal is its simplicity. It can be improvised almost anywhere by any number of players, and requires a simple, spherical ball rather than a specially shaped one. It has been played by people of limited stature, five feet or less, and occasionally those of excessive height or weight. And with the objective simply to score a goal between two posts, rolled up coats or other markers, its rules are simple.

Britain can claim to have developed and formalised the rules of association football which, by and large, still hold sway the world over. Yet prior to its adoption by the gentry in the nineteenth century the game enjoyed a reputation as the sport of hooligans and rabble-rousers, with the participants in the average game outnumbering the crowds at many English lower-division games today. Several fixtures in the early history of football attained the status of annual rituals; Ashbourne, Derbyshire, Dorset's Corfe Castle and Scone in

ABOVE Boys playing an informal game of football circa 1850

Scotland were among venues where an annual Shrove Tuesday fixture was observed.

When Cambridge University introduced the game into the curriculum at the turn of the seventeenth century, even its detractors had to reconsider. But with a welter of different rules proliferating, these games were strictly intramural affairs. With the advent

ABOVE A group of boys playing football in the mid 1850s when few rules prevailed

of the Industrial Revolution, few of the downtrodden working class had the time or energy to pursue such a physically demanding sport, and football passed into the hands of the leisured upper class.

Each school seemed to have its own special set of rules; at Rugby, handling (but not running in possession) was positively encouraged. Harrow played a recognisable form of today's game on grass, 11 players making up a team, while Winchester's goals extended the entire length of the goal line, like rugby's try line today. This situation would not last. The catalyst for change and stand-

ardisation was William Webb Ellis's legendary dash with the ball in 1823 that eventually gave rise to the game of rugby.

The face of football has never been changed quite so radically as on 26 October 1863, when 11 southern English clubs each sent representatives to London's Freemason's Tavern in the west central district of Holborn. Their intent was to thrash out a commonly acceptable form of rules by which the game of football could be played.

An annual general meeting of the Football Association, as it was termed, was set for the last week in September, roughly setting the beginning of the traditional season.

The rules agreed by the FA included the maximum length and breadth of the pitch, the procedures for kicking off and defined terms such as a goal, throw-in and offside. Corners were effectively free kicks, taken 15 yards from the goal line opposite where the ball went out of play. The rugby tactic of 'making a mark' (catching the ball and making a mark with the heel to claim a free kick) remained. Passing the ball by hand was permitted if caught 'fairly or on the first bounce'. Yet the rules were strangely non-specific in such matters as number of players, the penalty for foul play or even the shape of the ball. Such matters were to be decided by agreement between the captains.

Rudimentary and incomplete as these rules were in themselves, they had the immediate effect of stimulating

ball were soon abolished (save for the goalkeeper) and a tape was stretched between the posts (The first bar was introduced in 1882).

The first FA Cup Final was contested in 1872, before 2,000 paying spectators, by Wanderers and Royal Engineers. Wanderers managed just one goal, but it was enough. Within a few years, all clubs wished to take part – and by doing so accepted the FA rules of football which remain the basis by which the game is played throughout the world today. The dominant teams in the Cup's early years were the 'Gentlemen' or southerners, with Old Etonians (6), Wanderers (5), Royal Engineers and Oxford University (both 4) clocking up most Final appearances in the first dozen. Wanderers won the Cup in perpetuity after what remains one of only two hat-tricks of wins, between 1876 and 1878. The Cup was, however, returned to the Football Association on condition that no club could subsequently win it outright.

The teams had settled to 11 players apiece – and it was accepted that only one player on either side, the goalkeeper, could handle the ball. Corner kicks from the intersection

competition. An annual New Year fixture between Sheffield and Nottingham was inaugurated on 2 January 1865, Nottingham (now Notts County), the oldest current League club, having been founded three years earlier.

The game spread, no longer the exclusive preserve of the public schools yet by no means a working-class pastime. A crucial rule relaxed in 1867 was the provision that players in front of the ball were offside, thus reducing passing movements to lateral or backward directions. No wonder few goals were scored! This rule change took time to affect the pattern of play, which depended largely on individuals dribbling their way into a scoring position. Handling and catching the

ABOVE A drawing depicting opposing football teams sometime during the nineteenth century

of touch and goal-line were generally introduced in 1872, although the Sheffield clubs had been using these for four years or so previously. As with children's playground football, everyone wanted to be an attacker and the goalkeeper was typically covered by, at most, two defenders.

It was the Scots who first discovered the opportunities this offered, and their emphasis on team play saw them advance apace. They were also assisted by playing to consistent rules. The 2-3-5 formation evolved, with three of the forwards now dropping deeper as half-backs to provide an extra line of defence where necessary. The centre-half acted as the supply route to the front line. This 'pyramid' style of play was employed by the Double (League and FA Cup)-winning Preston team in the League's first season,

LEFT A goal is scored during an inter-university match between Oxford and Cambridge, around 1875

and their success spoke for itself.

One major problem with the offside rule was exploited by Newcastle defender Billy McCracken. He would move forward to play his opponents offside, knowing that there was still a covering man as well as the goalkeeper to foil the attacker even if he mistimed his run – which was not often. The law was changed so that players had to be between the man in possession and his opponents' goal line when the ball was played – a situation that left the defenders far less margin for error. In the season following the law change, the goal tally for the League's divisions rose from 4,700 to 6,373.

Penalties were introduced in September 1891 as a result of an incident during an FA Cup quarter-final between Notts County and Stoke at Trent Bridge. County's Hendry produced an acrobatic goalkeeping save – unfortunately, however, he was the left-back. A free kick was awarded on the goal line, but goalkeeper Toone saved the point-blank shot. Since County's 1-0 win meant they reached the semi-final and later the Final, a public outcry provoked a change in the laws.

While football was changing its rules and regulations, playing kit was undergoing its own metamorphosis. In the 1870s, for instance, a match programme was essential for player identification, the colour of stockings or cap being the only differentiating feature between

men of the same team. Although numbering was not introduced until 1933, caps had long since fallen into disuse.

Stimulated by the 1866 game with Sheffield, the London-based Football Association determined to expand the game's influence into a wider area.

Sheffield themselves joined in 1867, and other teams were quick to follow suit. The amazing expansion of the 1870s was due primarily to the effort of one Charles Alcock, elected at the age of 28 as Secretary of the Association. He devised the idea of international competition, inaugurating an annual England-Scotland fixture.

Meanwhile, Alcock had devised the ideal method of encouraging competitive play: the Football Association Cup, purchased for the princely sum of £20. Fifteen clubs entered for the 1871-72 competition, though one – Donington Grammar School in Lincolnshire – withdrew without playing a game. Queen's Park, who contributed a guinea to the cost of the trophy, were lucky enough to draw Donington – then, thanks to a lopsided draw, contest the semi-finals without having had to play a single qualifying game.

Their semi-final against Wanderers (the team of which Alcock was secretary, and formerly known as Forest) was played in London, as indeed were all semis and Finals for the first years. The two teams could not break the goalless deadlock, and with extra time and penalty shootouts not yet devised, the

RIGHT A reprint of
'The Rules of
Association Football
1863' which
documents the
thirteen original
rules of soccer as
written by Oxbridge
graduates, and
represents the first
recording of the
fundamental tenets
of football

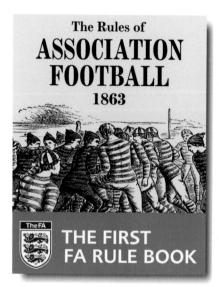

RIGHT A reprint of 'The Rules of Association Football 1863' which documents the thirteen original rules of soccer as written by Oxbridge graduates, and represents the first recording of the fundamental tenets of football

the team he'd represented previously. This was a significant loss, for Kinnaird was clearly the outstanding player of the era. He won five Cup winner's medals, as well as one cap for Scotland. After retiring from playing, he served as FA President for some 33 years.

Soon after the second defeat, Wanderers retired from competitive football completely. It was well that they did, for the game was about to be taken over by the 'professors', professional footballers from Scotland who lent their talents to such northern teams as Darwen, Sheffield Wednesday and Bolton. Professionalism reflected the industrial nature of the North, where leisure time was at a premium. The match that signified the end of the Gentlemen's monopoly was the Cup Final of 1882 when Blackburn became the first northern club to make it to the last stage of the contest. They were unlucky to lose 1-0 to Old Etonians, and indeed had been tipped to win.

It may seem far-fetched, but the founder of the English Football League was not only a Scotsman but a man who never played a game of first-class

Scots withdrew, being unable to manage the 800-mile round trip to Glasgow and back for the replay.

The demise of Wanderers as strongest of the Gentlemen teams was mirrored by the rise of the public schools' 'old boy' teams. Two Old Etonians victories over them in 1878-79 and 1879-80 marked the turning of the tide. Their most famous player Arthur (later Lord) Kinnaird, a future FA President, chose to play for his old school rather than

football in his entire life. Perthshire gentleman William McGregor was the prime mover behind two meetings held in the spring of 1888 in London and Manchester involving the 12 football clubs who were to become the League's founder members. The London meeting took place on 22 March 1888 at Anderton's Hotel in London, on the eve of that year's Cup Final. The clubs' revenue depended on a good Cup run: an early exit could be financially disastrous. This new competition guaranteed fixtures and revenue for the country's top dozen teams, split equally between the North and the Midlands; the South of England remained a stronghold of the amateur game.

Preston North End were the first Champions in the season 1888-89, with Aston Villa runners-up. So dominant were Preston, in fact, that they achieved the League and Cup double. What wrote their name into the record books, however, was the fact that they were undefeated in the League and did not concede a Cup goal – a record that seems likely never to be broken.

Preston also won the League the following year, despite four defeats, with Everton second – a foretaste of things to come, since the positions were reversed in the 1890-91 season. Preston claimed runners-up spot for three seasons running, underlining their claim to be the first major force in League football. That last season saw the 12 founder members become 14 with the addition of Stoke and Darwen.

The original intention was that League points should be awarded solely for wins. But after 10 weeks of the first season, this was amended to make drawn games yield one point apiece as compared to two for a win – a system that remained in operation until 1981-82, when the proliferation of

RIGHT The Scottish
FA Cup winners
Renton in 1888

goalless draws encouraged the League to improve the points for a win to three.

'Proud' Preston's mantle was donned in the 1890s by Sunderland, who took the League title in the seasons 1891-92, 1892-93 and again in 1894-95, having finished second to Aston Villa in the intervening season. Their success stoked the fires of football fervour in the North East, where the industrial base provided by shipbuilding supplied both the men to play football and the crowds to watch.

The team also included a Scots contingent, drawn southwards across the border in search of fame and fortune. One of these, goalkeeper Ned Doig, played against West Bromwich on 20 September 1890 before his transfer from Arbroath had been formally registered, costing his new club two points. He proved a worthwhile buy in the long term, however. In seven seasons, the team were beaten only once at Roker Park. Sunderland were known as the 'Team of All the Talents'.

In 1892-93, their first Championship campaign, they topped 100 goals for the first time in League history, being assisted by the expansion of the division to 16 clubs. This feat was not to be

equalled until the interwar years when West Bromwich notched 104 goals in a 22-club division. Sunderland had not, in fact, been one of the founding 12, but

until 1958. By then, they had added another three Championships to their 1890s successes.

Aston Villa from the Midlands were to monopolise the title from 1895-96 to the end of the century, save a single win (in 1897-98) by Sheffield United. The latter had joined the League in 1893, a year after their city rivals Wednesday.

The League had added a 12-strong Second Division for the season 1892-93, simultaneously adding a further two teams to the First. The lower echelon had previously been known as the Football Alliance, a competition set up in 1889 by a group of non-League teams which had shown its collective class by drawing in a representative match with a League XI. The promotion and relegation issues were to be settled by a series of three test matches. As a result Sheffield United and Darwen were promoted, with Notts County – one of the founding 12 – relegated. (This arrangement was, of course, all but duplicated in the 1980s when play-offs were introduced.)

The system was dispensed with after an 1898 fixture between Stoke and Burnley which ended in a goalless draw – coincidentally or otherwise, a result

their history was impressive enough. Added to the League strength in 1890 when Stoke temporarily dropped out, they retained their First Division place

BELOW Huge crowds
at the 1901 FA
Cup Final between
Tottenham Hotspur
and Sheffield United
at Crystal Palace

that kept both clubs in the top flight. Thereafter, an automatic two up/two down system of promotion and relegation was instituted. This was modified to three-up, three-down in 1973-74, the third place being made the subject of a play-off in 1986-87. The new division had failed to admit a single club from the south: that had to wait until the election of Woolwich Arsenal to the Second

BELOW Huge crowds at the 1901 FA Cup Final between Tottenham Hotspur and Sheffield United at Crystal Palace

Division in 1893. By 1894-95 there were 16 clubs in each division.

The League and Cup Double has remained a cherished dream for First Division clubs: only one team managed to repeat Preston's inaugural feat before the end of the century. Aston Villa achieved the distinction in 1897 as part of the four Championships in five seasons that rounded off the decade and indeed the century. The magnitude of their feat is underlined by the fact that the runners-up Sheffield United trailed a full 11 points behind. No-one would emulate their achievement for fully 64 years until the Spurs team of 1960-61 recorded the first Double of the modern era.

Beating Liverpool with ease 3-0 in the semi-final, Villa faced their Merseyside rivals at Crystal Palace, defeating them 3-2 to add the Cup to the League prize already secured. One of the powerhouses of this team was half-back John Reynolds, an international for both England and Ireland (though born in Blackburn). Villa had won the Cup two years earlier, defeating West Bromwich by a single goal at the first Crystal Palace Final. The Cup won in Double year was a different one since, after lending it to sports outfitter William Shillcock for display in his window, they never saw it again.

The FA Cup provided surprises in the following two years. In 1900, non-League Southampton battled to the Final before being dispatched in no uncertain fashion, 4-0, by Bury of the First Division. The following year, however, saw even more of a shock when Tottenham Hotspur became the first – and still the only – non-League club to win the Cup since 1888. They took two games to defeat Sheffield United, 3-1 after a 2-2 draw at Crystal Palace.

One of the main reasons the game of football took off in Scotland in preference to rugby may well be the fact that well-grassed areas were few and far between, especially in the Scottish lowlands. Soccer could be – and frequently was – improvised anywhere and everywhere. On 9 July 1867 the Queen's Park Football Club was founded in Glasgow, where there were only three parks to alleviate the need to play on cobbles.

Over the three years following their formation, Queen's Park were to attract Scotland's best players to their ranks, dominating the Scottish scene. The establishment of international matches with England broadened their horizons and they soon joined the FA to take part in the first FA Cup competitions. As recorded earlier, they did so with some success, reaching two Finals before the newly-formed Scottish Football Association outlawed their participation in 1887. Their opponents in each case were Blackburn Rovers, the scores 2-1 and 2-0.

Queen's Park's total dominance of football north of the border can be gauged by the fact that all but two of the team that met England in the first international on Scottish soil on 30 November 1872 were from the club. The gate receipts from the match, a goalless draw, were £200, with the 4,000 spectators each charged one shilling admission. Such untold riches encouraged Queen's Park to seek larger accommodation, which became available in the shape of Hampden Park. This is still the home of Queen's Park FC and the venue at which Scotland's international matches are played.

It was obvious that forming a Scottish equivalent to the English FA would stimulate competition for places in the national side, while playing teams

LEFT The players of Tottenham Hotspur Football Club with the 'Sheriff of London' shield trophy in 1902

ABOVE J Crawford of Scottish League team Queen's Park, 1931

nearer home would make life a lot easier for Queen's Park. If proof were needed, one only had to recall that in 1872 and 1873, the first two years of the FA Cup, the Scots had been obliged to scratch at the semi-final stage (the first time after forcing a draw) through lack of funds.

Thus it was that 1873 saw the formation of the eight-team Scottish FA. Such was Queen's Park's continuing superiority that it was not until

16 January 1875 that an opponent even managed to score against them, the team in question being Vale of Leven. Elsewhere, standards were equally uneven: the legendary 36-0 win by Arbroath against Bon Accord in 1885 still stands as the record British first-class football score.

As with Queen's Park, the clubs affiliated to the Scottish FA could, in the early years, compete against English clubs or even be members of both English and Scottish bodies. This was, however, soon to change, the catalyst being the advent of professionalism in England. The Scottish FA chose to bar 68 Scots playing south of the border, regarding professionalism as 'evil'. Queen's Park, who today remain the only Scottish League club to have amateur status, were in the forefront of this crusade. Clashes in the 1886-87 FA Cup exacerbated the situation, and Rangers, who went out to Aston Villa in the semi-final held at Crewe, were to be the last Scottish club to venture south.

International matches, of course, continued, with Scotland having by far the upper hand, notching seven wins and two draws in the 11 fixtures since that first Glasgow game. This dominance owed much to Queen's Park's players reproducing club form for their country – as indeed one would expect when the players concerned made up the majority of the team.

The SFA edict that clubs should not belong to any other national organisation nor compete in their competitions meant a Scottish League was desperately needed. Such a body was formed in 1890 and was, as one would expect, initially proudly amateur. Dumbarton and Rangers shared the first Championship, drawing in a play-off game – the only such occasion in the history of the League. Dumbarton emerged to take the title outright the following season.

The inevitable quickening of the southwards migration from the all-amateur Scottish game led to another rash of expulsions. The annual internationals were proving something of a headache, however, since Scotland refused to pick the 'exiles' and inevitably suffered for their pains. A 5-2 drubbing in 1893 at Richmond was the turning point – and when Celtic, that year's Champions, moved a motion to accept professionalism in the Scottish League the old guard was routed.

Queen's Park, who had not joined the League, found it impossible to maintain their leading position and despite swallowing their pride and joining the League in 1899 they were never to scale such heights again.

The 1893 team to play England was divided 5-4 between Queen's Park – the team of the past – and Celtic, one of the two teams of the future. Even though the Scottish League grew swiftly – after its first season it could claim the affiliation of 64 clubs in associated leagues – it was thenceforth to be dominated by the two Glasgow clubs, Rangers and Celtic.

The 'Old Firm's domination was broken only 13 times by outside clubs between the advent of professionalism in 1893-94 and the introduction of a new three-division system in 1974. (There is currently a Premier League and three lower divisions.) A Second Division was established in 1893, although promotion and relegation between the two divisions was far from automatic.

Back in England, the venue of the FA Cup Final had settled at Crystal Palace in 1895, having moved northwards from the Oval, with its limited 25,000 capacity, to Fallowfield, Manchester in 1893. This arrangement proved disastrous, and Goodison Park, Merseyside was a more successful venue in 1894 before a permanent home for the fixture was found at Crystal Palace. Crowds approached 100,000, a figure achieved in 1905 when Aston Villa beat Newcastle United in the latter's first Double attempt. This was only the second time a match had attracted this figure, the first being 1901 when 114,815 attended. The Football Association introduced extra time in 1913 as a method to decide the destination of the Cup at the first attempt. But the FA Cup Final would reside at the Palace only until the outbreak of World War I.

Newcastle United, feeding off the north-east hotbed of football fervour, dominated the upper reaches of the Football League at this time, yet though their achievements were noteworthy they couldn't quite follow through. They first stood on the threshold of the League and Cup Double in 1905, but a 0-2 Cup Final reverse against Aston Villa dashed their hopes of adding it to the League Championship. In 1906 they could only finish fourth, running

up in the Cup again to Everton. In 1907 came another Championship win, though an early Cup defeat against non-League opposition proved hard to swallow. 1908 saw a repeat of 1906, losing 3-1 to Wolves. The League followed the year after and in 1910 they finally won the Cup.

Aston Villa had taken two League Championships at the end of the decade (and century), but apart from Sheffield Wednesday's consecutive League wins in 1902-03 and 1903-04, the title changed hands with surprising regularity. Oldham nearly capped their brief period in the top flight with a Championship win, losing out in the final game of the 1914-15 season, the last before war halted competition.

Chapter 2

The First Golden Age

AS FOOTBALL RESUMED AFTER the First World War the English game was very insular, and would remain so for another three decades. This was partly because it was more advanced in technical and organisational terms than Europe, and partly because international travel was much more primitive. (Ironically, it would be English coaches, like Jimmy Hogan who, either side of the First World War, helped the European game to develop to the point where it was at least the equal of the English.) An insular mentality may also have been a contributory factor.

The Home International Championship was the major international tournament, the clash between England and Scotland the main game. There was also the occasional close season tour of Europe. For players like Bob Crompton, therefore, to win 41 caps implied an international career that stretched over a dozen or so seasons. Confidence that all was well with English football at international level came with success in the 1908 and 1912 Olympic Games, when the gold medal for football was twice won comfortably by British teams. But the apparent superiority of the English game proved to be illusory.

The inter-war period was something of a contradiction for English football. The Football League and FA Cup competitions were even more popular

FAR LEFT
Bob Crompton of
Blackburn Rovers
and England

LEFT Scott Duncan
(left), manager
of Ipswich Town
football club, and
Jimmy Hogan,
manager of Aston
Villa, before an FA
Cup tie replay, 1939

than in the pre-1914 period, a critical change in the laws tried to make the game more open and attacking, and a national stadium was acquired. More worrying, however, was the fact that the insularity of the English game was becoming exposed. Not only did the FA decline to take part in either of the first two World Cup competitions, but the technical frailties of the England team at international level were also starting to become apparent.

Immediately on the resumption of the League programme in 1919, a third division was created out of the Southern League. A fourth division followed 12 months later, the two new divisions becoming the Third South and Third North. Only the Champions were promoted to Division Two and the bottom clubs were subject to re-election at the League's AGM each year rather than to automatic demotion.

Thus, the 12-club, one-division League of 1888 had grown to two divisions and 40 clubs by 1914. By the second inter-war season there were 88 clubs competing in four equal-size divisions, which is how it remained through to 1939. Professional League football was in effect extended to all parts of England and Wales, becoming a truly national game.

The inter-war League campaigns were dominated by two clubs, Huddersfield in the 1920s and Arsenal in the 1930s. Both managed hat-tricks of League titles, and were also runners-up on other occasions, the first signs that the First Division title was becoming a private competition between a relatively small number of clubs. In the 20 inter-war seasons, there were just ten different winners of the League Championship, five of whom won it on more than one occasion.

The FA Cup, on the other hand, was won by 16 different clubs in this period and only three clubs won it more than once. As well as the Terriers and the Gunners, six clubs (Newcastle, West Brom, Everton, Manchester City, Sheffield Wednesday and Sunderland) won both competitions in these years.

Huddersfield Town had risen without trace to become the major power in English football in the decade immediately following the First World War. Yet only two months into the new era, in November 1919, Huddersfield were faced by a financial crisis that threatened them with a transfer to nearby Leeds, whose club had been expelled from the League the previous month for financial irregularities. Local support saved the club which, remarkably, went on to win promotion from the Second Division that season and to make the FA Cup Final, only to lose to Aston Villa at Stamford Bridge. From these turbulent beginnings, the Terriers soared to new heights.

ABOVE The players
of Huddersfield
Town, 1927

The appointment of Herbert Chapman as manager in March 1921 was a turning point. The FA Cup was won the following month when Preston were beaten by a penalty, and the League Championship went to Leeds Road in three consecutive seasons between 1923 and 1926. By the time the hat-trick was completed, Chapman had been enticed to Arsenal, but the team was good enough to survive his departure. In 1926-27, Huddersfield

RIGHT
Herbert Chapman,
the Arsenal manager
(left), was the leading
inter-war club
supremo

were runners-up in the League, and 12 months later they again finished second and lost at Wembley to Blackburn. Under Clem Stephenson, the club had two more losing Wembley appearances in the interwar period, to Arsenal in 1930 and ironically, to Preston in 1938, by a penalty.

Chapman's new club, Arsenal, dominated the 1930s to an extent only Liverpool in the 1980s and Manchester United in the 1990s have since matched. The first signs of stirring in North London came in 1927, when the Gunners reached their first FA Cup Final, only to lose to the softest of goals.

This was the team that Herbert Chapman built, bankrolled initially by the club's controversial chairman, Sir Henry Norris, and it got better. He bought big, with the likes of Alex James and David Jack and, more modestly, paying relatively small sums for such outstanding players as Eddie Hapgood, Cliff Bastin and Joe Hulme.

The first honour was won in 1930, when Arsenal defeated Chapman's former club Huddersfield 2-0 to lift the FA Cup at Wembley. The victory marked the ending of the 1920s and the start of the 1930s in more senses

than one. The first Football League Championship followed 12 months later, with 66 points, a new record. A near Double in 1931-32, runners-up in

both League and Cup, was followed by a hat-trick of League titles.

Half-way through this sequence, Chapman died, but it was business as usual under his successor, BBC commentator George Allison, whose first signing was Ted Drake. A fifth Championship was unexpectedly won in 1937-38, with just 52 points, the lowest for a side finishing top in a 42-match campaign, but not before a second Wembley triumph, against Sheffield United in 1936.

Yet the First Division was still more open than the Premiership is today. During the 1920s and 1930s, only three clubs, Arsenal, Liverpool and Sunderland, had unbroken membership of the top flight. And fortunes could turn very quickly. Everton, Champions in 1928, finished bottom of the table two years later. The Toffees, however, bounced straight back as Second Division Champions in 1930-31 and remarkably reclaimed the League title the following year. Manchester City, Champions in 1936-37, were relegated 12 months later, despite being the First Division's highest scorers. West Brom, Burnley, Newcastle and Sheffield Wednesday, Champions during the 1920s, all suffered the indignity of relegation a few years later.

The Cup provided much of the footballing glamour of the period.

For the first three inter-war seasons, however, the FA Cup was virtually homeless, using Chelsea's Stamford Bridge to stage the Final. Then, in 1923, Wembley played host for the first time. Built for the Empire Exhibition, it was acquired by Arthur Elvin and used for most of England's Home Internationals and all Cup Finals until 2000.

By the end of the twentieth century, however, Wembley was tired and the facilities compared unfavourably with many modern club grounds. But those flickering cinematic images of the first game, the 1923 FA Cup Final between Bolton and West Ham, are among the most immediately recognisable of football scenes. An official crowd of 126,000 saw some of the match, which Bolton won 2-0, although unofficial estimates put the real figure closer to 200,000.

The elegant David Jack scored Wembley's first goal which helped Bolton to the first of three FA Cup victories in six years, achieved without conceding a goal in any Final. It was the first of many memorable Cup moments associated with the new stadium. Upsets are the essence of Cup football and Cardiff's victory over Arsenal in 1927 (by a soft goal con-

ceded by Welsh keeper Dan Lewis) and Blackburn's 1928 triumph over the then mighty Huddersfield were among the biggest surprises. In 1931, West Brom completed a double of sorts, winning the Cup and promotion from Division Two in the same season.

The following year saw one of Wembley's most controversial moments when Newcastle's Allen scored against Arsenal from a cross after the ball had clearly crossed the by-line. The teenage Frank Swift fainting at the final whistle in 1934, the drama of Sheffield Wednesday's two late, late goals against West Brom in 1935, the tension of George Mutch's last-minute penalty for Preston against Huddersfield in 1938 and finally Jack Tinn's spats and Portsmouth's unlikely triumph over Wolves in the last peacetime Final are all enduring parts of Wembley legend.

Through the work of English coaches like Jimmy Hogan, continental football had made great strides, although the English public was quite unaware of these developments. Between 1919 and 1929, the English national side played exactly 50 internationals, two-thirds of which were Home Internationals. The only 'overseas' countries played were Belgium, France, Sweden, Luxembourg and Spain. Not until May 1930 did England and Germany meet in a full international and another three years passed before the first meeting with Italy.

Although the unbeaten home record against overseas teams was somehow preserved until 1953, inter-war sides had their share of defeats on their travels. Spain were the first to inflict pain, in May 1929, when England lost 4-3 in Madrid. Austria, where Jimmy Hogan was such an influence, man-

LEFT Arsenal's Wilf Copping, Eddie Hapgood, George Male, Ted Drake, and Cliff Bastin, all of whom were regulars with the England team

THE FIRST GOLDEN AGE

aged to hold England to a goalless draw in Vienna in 1930 and then came very close to winning at Stamford Bridge in December 1932. In the end, the hosts scraped a 4-3 win.

Even in the Home Internationals, England did not enjoy unchallenged supremacy. Perhaps Scotland's finest hour was the 5-1 drubbing the Wembley Wizards handed out to England in 1928, when a tiny forward line of Jackson, Dunn, Gallacher, James and Morton destroyed England on a rain-soaked Wembley pitch. In the 1930s, moreo-

ver, England won the title outright just once, while Wales managed three wins.

There were, nevertheless, some heroic performances, in particular the triumphs over Italy in 1934 and Germany in 1938, victories over the two leading fascist nations which were welcomed for political as well as sporting reasons. For the match against reigning World Champions Italy at Highbury in November 1934, the English side contained seven Arsenal players (Moss, Male, Hapgood, Copping, Bowden, Drake and Bastin). It was a brutal encounter from which England emerged 3-2 winners.

Success against Germany came in Berlin in May 1938, at a time when war seemed increasingly likely. Humiliatingly, but on the advice of the British Embassy, the England team gave the Nazi salute beforehand, but it was the only respect they showed the hosts. In an inspired performance, England ran out 6-3 winners. Yet seven days later, exactly the same England team lost 2-1 to Switzerland in Zurich which showed the flaws in the national side. In an era of so many talented individuals, it was a puzzle that the national side did not do better.

Jimmy Hogan's unfortunate managerial experiences in England highlighted some of the technical shortcomings which became even more apparent in the post-war era, but which were already evident in the limited exposure the national team had to continental opposition. Just like the 5-1 victory over Germany in the autumn of 2001, the stunning 6-3 success in Berlin in 1938 was a false dawn. The day of football reckoning might have been delayed by the war, but it was just around the corner.

ABOVE The English and German football teams coming onto the field before a game in Berlin, while some players give the Nazi salute, 1938

Chapter 3

The Post-War Boom

BRITAIN'S FOOTBALL-LOVING PUBLIC was largely starved of competitive action between 1939 and 1946. During the early days of the war friendly matches were played, but these attracted little interest. Regional leagues were then set up, but the public response was not always terribly enthusiastic. However, the cessation of hostilities was to herald a tremendous boom time for the game.

The 1939-40 season had been brought to a premature close in the September. Most English sides had played just three games and Blackpool were top of the First (top) Division, having taken a maximum six points from their three fixtures. The Scots had started the season earlier, and Rangers headed Division 'A' having secured four wins and a draw.

When the old system was re-established in season 1946-47, Rangers won the Scottish title, finishing two points clear of Hibs, while Liverpool were English Champions, finishing just one point clear of Manchester United and Wolves.

In the immediate post-war years, football grounds were very different from those of today. There were no executive boxes (there would have been few executives to fill them) and only the comparatively wealthy chose to sit in the stands.

Apart from going to the cinema and watching football, there was little else going on in the world of entertainment – and football was cheap. You could gain access to many grounds for as little as one shilling and threepence (6p) and a programme might cost you 2d or 3d (about 1p). Facilities were basic, and

it is also true that wages were very low, but football was a lot cheaper in real terms than it is today.

And so working men went to football in their tens of thousands. The leading First Division (top-flight) sides attracted crowds in excess of 40,000, week in and week out. The ending of Saturday morning working helped, too.

The average attendance at Wolves'

THE POST-WAR BOOM

BELOW Sheffield Wednesday fans worriedly watching a game from the terraces, 1940

Molineux ground in 1946-47 was 43,000, while Chelsea attracted an average of 46,363 in season 1948-49 and Sunderland an average of 47,785 in 1949-50. Even a modest side playing in the English Second Division could expect regular gates in excess of 20,000. In 1949-50 Sheffield Wednesday's average gate was 40,692 and when Manchester City played Fulham in a Division Two fixture in January 1947, a remarkable 47,658 turned up to watch. Norwich City, playing in Division Three (South) had an average attendance of 23,624 in 1950-51.

In 1946-47, total attendance figures for first-class football reached 35 million. In 1947-48 it rose to 40 million, generating an income of £4,000,000 – an average of two shillings (10p) per head. The figures include attendances at FA Cup games, internationals and some of the minor leagues, but in 1948-49 more than 41 million people watched League matches alone. This total has never been surpassed.

Footballers were stars and heroes then, as they are today. They were quite well paid by the standards of the time but, until the abolition of the maximum wage in 1961, their wages were very modest by comparison with the stars of stage and screen. After the war, League footballers were entitled to be paid, in addition to their basic wage, a bonus of two pounds for a win, and one pound for a draw. These bonuses were later doubled: riches indeed! When Jimmy Hill, as leader of the players' union, began his campaign for the removal of the maximum wage, it stood at £20 a week (it had been as little as £12 a week in 1947).

To a large extent, English football after the war was very similar to the

BELOW Sheffield Wednesday fans worriedly watching a game from the terraces, 1940

Having won the title at the end of the first post-war season, Liverpool were not to win it again until 1963-64. Portsmouth won the First Division Championship in 1948-49, and again the following season when they beat Wolves to the title on goal average.

Two clubs dominated the Scottish Division 'A' after the war: Rangers and Hibernian. Rangers won the Scottish Championship four times and Hibs won it thrice, before Celtic topped the table at the end of season 1953-54.

In England, two clubs dominated the First Division in the 1950s: Manchester United and Wolverhampton Wanderers. Manchester United won the First Division title in 1951-52, 1955-56 and 1956-57. They also won it at the end of 1964-65. Wolves, led by England captain and centre-half Billy Wright, won the First Division title in 1953-54, 1957-58 and 1958-59. Other teams to

LEFT Jimmy Hill whose campaign for higher earnings led to a wages explosion

game that had been played in the 1930s. Arsenal had won the First Division title five times between 1930-31 and 1938-39, and had won it three times on the trot in 1932-33, 1933-34 and 1934-35. After the war, their fortunes faded a little, although they did win the League title in 1947-48 and again in 1952-53 – their last League Championship until they achieved the League and Cup Double in 1970-71.

THE POST-WAR BOOM

RIGHT Johnny Carey, the Manchester United captain, leads his team out onto the pitch

BELOW Some of the crowd watching an FA Cup match at the Wolverhampton Wanderers football ground, 1949

win the title during this period included Tottenham Hotspur in 1950-51 and 1960-61 (their Double-winning year) and Chelsea, who topped the First Division table in 1954-55.

FA Cup-winning sides have often experienced a mediocre season in the League. This was not the case for Derby County when they beat Charlton Athletic 4-1 in the 1946 Final – because there had been no League season! However, when Charlton took their revenge on the Twin Towers of Wembley the following year, beating Burnley by a goal to nil, they only managed 19th place in the First Division. The most successful FA Cup side of the 1940s through to the early 1960s was Newcastle United. They won the trophy three times – in 1951, 1952 and 1955. Manchester United (1948 and 1963),

Tottenham Hotspur (1961 and 1962) and Wolves (1949 and 1960) each won it twice.

Between 1947 and 1964 the Scottish FA Cup was won seven times by Rangers, three times each by Aberdeen and Celtic, and once each by Motherwell, Hearts, Falkirk, Clyde and St. Mirren. Overall, there is no doubt that Rangers were the dominant Scottish club side of the immediate post-war period.

Manchester United were arguably the English team of the 1950s but they were to suffer a disaster of horrific proportions in February 1958, when a plane bringing them home after a European game in Yugoslavia crashed, in icy conditions, on take-off at Munich airport.

Their manager, Matt (later Sir Matt)

Busby, had built a magnificent young team which would undoubtedly have won many more honours, but the side was decimated by the crash. Geoffrey Bent, Roger Byrne, Edward Colman, Duncan Edwards, David Pegg, Mark Jones, Billy Whelan and Tommy Taylor all lost their lives, as did Frank Swift, the former Manchester City and England goalkeeper, who was by now a journalist. Matt Busby himself received injuries so serious that it seemed unlikely that he would recover, but recover he did – and he went on to build another team.

BELOW The wreckage of the plane that was carrying the 1958 Manchester United team

Chapter 4

England's Finest Hour

EVEN IF THEY ARE TOO YOUNG TO remember it personally, every supporter of England's national team has to admit their finest hour remains the World Cup victory over West Germany at Wembley in 1966. It not only set the seal on very nearly a century of international competition, but has presented a punishing benchmark for successive teams and managers to live up to.

England's first seven international fixtures were against Scotland. The series began on 30 November 1872 when 4,000 expectant Scotsmen saw the countries play out a goalless draw at Hamilton Crescent, Glasgow. Undeterred by this less than promising start, England invited the Scots to compete again, this time at the Kennington Oval in March 1873. About 3,000 Englishmen were no doubt thrilled by a 4-2 victory for the home team.

After five more international fixtures against Scotland, the English invited Wales to the Oval in January 1879, when the visitors were beaten 2-1. Ireland were beaten 13-0 in Belfast in 1882, but the home international series, as such, did not get under way until the 1883-84 season.

England's first match against 'foreign' opposition did not come until 1908, when Austria were beaten 6-1 in Vienna on 6 June. The fixture was repeated two days later, and this time England won 11-1, with four goals from Viv Woodward and three from Tom Bradshaw. Two days after that, England were in Budapest, beating Hungary 7-0, and George Hilsdon scored four of them.

There were fewer big wins after World War I. Still, in March 1923 England beat Belgium 6-1 at Highbury, and in May 1927 they beat them again, this time 9-1. Dixie Dean scored a hat-trick in that match and, ten days later, he scored

BELOW Players competing for the ball during an England versus Scotland football match at the Oval, 1878

BELOW A G Bower of
England (left) shakes
hands with Belgium's
Captain Swaertenbroecks
before the start of the
international match,
1924

another in a 5-2 victory in Luxembourg. He only scored two when England beat France 6-0 in Paris on 25 May.

In December 1931 England beat Spain 7-1 at Highbury. Dean managed only a single goal but John Smith, Joe Johnson and Sam Crooks scored two apiece. By 1934 cracks were beginning to show. Even with the likes of Eddie Hapgood and Cliff Bastin in the team, England were beaten 2-1 in both Hungary and Czechoslovakia. Their home record was still very good but more war clouds heralded a dark time ahead for English international football.

Officially, wartime football came to an end at the start of the 1946-47 League season. Many players had, sadly, lost their best years to the conflict but many were also to make their names in internationals played during the late 1940s.

Walter Winterbottom became the England manager in 1946. He came in for a fair amount of criticism during his long reign, but his record of 79 victories, 32 draws and 28 defeats in 139 international matches, was far

BELOW A G Bower of England (left) shakes hands with Belgium's Captain Swaertenbroecks before the start of the international match, 1924

from a bad one. He had played for Manchester United, where he made just 27 appearances as a half-back (midfielder) before spinal problems forced him into early retirement in 1938.

Winterbottom was only 33 when he took over the England team. He was a very good coach, and as well as establishing a national coaching scheme, he also set up England's youth and Under-23 teams. He was probably hampered by the fact that, although he was manager, teams were still chosen by a committee.

Winterbottom had inherited some excellent players after the war. His, and England's, first postwar 'official' international was a Home Championship match in Northern Ireland, played on 28 September 1946. It resulted in a 7-2 victory for the visitors, with Wilf Mannion scoring a hat-trick.

The internationals played during the late 1940s were all either against the home countries, or friendlies against European opposition. One notable result came in a game against Italy in Turin, during May 1948. With Tom Finney playing on the left wing and Matthews on the right, England ran out 4-0 winners. Their scorers were

Finney (2), Lawton and Mortensen.

When Uruguay had won the World Cup in 1930, and Italy had won it in 1934 and again in 1938, England had

ABOVE
Walter Winterbottom, England's first manager

not bothered to enter the competition. This was almost certainly a mistake so, when the year 1950 was selected for the re-start of the competition, England decided to put in an appearance. The

1950 World Cup Finals were held in Brazil, and England started brightly enough by beating Chile 2-0 (Mortensen and Mannion). The Brazilians were well on the way to emerging as a great

team, and would later reach the Final, but England were inexplicably beaten 1-0 by the USA and then, also 1-0, by Spain. Even with the likes of Billy Wright, Tom Finney and Stan Mortensen in the side, it was clear that England was no longer the supreme footballing nation.

In November 1953, Ferenc Puskas and his Mighty Magyars overcame England at Wembley. The 6-3 scoreline stunned everyone, no-one more than England right-back Alf Ramsey. Hungary won the return fixture 7-1, and then England made another early exit from the World Cup. They drew 4-4 with Belgium, beat the host nation, Switzerland, 2-0 in Berne, and then went down 4-2 to Uruguay at the quarter-final stage.

The European Nations Cup did not get underway until 1960 (and even then, England decided not to enter) and so it was only in the World Cup that the side could seriously test its strength against other nations. It usually did well in the qualifying matches, and this was again the case prior to the 1958 Finals. Having beaten Denmark twice and the Republic of Ireland once, Winterbottom's boys journeyed to Sweden full of hope, and began their campaign in the Finals with a 2-2 draw against the USSR. This was followed by a creditable goalless draw with Brazil, and a rather less creditable 2-2 draw with Austria. Three draws were not enough to secure a place in the quarter-finals, and a play-off with the USSR was lost by a goal to nil.

By the end of the 1950s everyone knew that England were no longer the kings of the game – even though they did defeat a depleted Scotland side 9-3 in April 1961, with a hat-trick from Jimmy Greaves and a couple each from Bobby Smith and Johnny Haynes. Walter Winterbottom was to have one last go at real glory in 1962, when his team travelled to Chile. England managed to scrape into the quarter-finals, where they lost 3-1 to Brazil.

It was time for Walter to quit his post, and in January 1963 Alf Ramsey became England manager. Ramsey, born in

ABOVE World Cup match between England and the United States, 1950

occasions. As manager of Ipswich, he had guided the Suffolk club from Division Three (South) to the championship of the top division in just five years, a quite remarkable achievement. Ramsey was the first full-time England manager and, crucially, was given total control over team selection.

Ramsey's first game in charge was a European Nations Cup qualifying match in Paris. It resulted in a 5-2 defeat at the hands of France, and, as the teams had drawn 1-1 in Sheffield before he took over, it meant that England were out of the competition at the first attempt. Ramsey's second game also resulted in defeat, this time by Scotland (2-1) at Wembley, but during the remainder of 1963 his side went seven games without losing.

Over the next two years, Ramsey began building a team for an assault on the Jules Rimet Trophy in 1966. The World Cup Finals were to be played in England, so the host nation qualified automatically. This meant the manager could experiment and, during 1964, players such as Gordon Banks, Ray Wilson, Bobby Moore, Roger Hunt and Bobby Charlton made regular appearances. In 1965, they were joined

Dagenham on 22 January 1920, had served Southampton and Tottenham and played for his country on 32

by Jack Charlton, Alan Ball and Nobby Stiles. Only Geoff Hurst had yet to come to prominence.

England were to play a total of 17 matches during 1966. The second, a friendly against West Germany which England won 1-0 at Wembley featured nine of the players who were to feature in the World Cup Final later in the year. By contrast, only five West Germans – goalkeeper Hans Tilkowski, plus Willi Schulz, Wolfgang Weber, Franz Beckenbauer and Siegfried Held – were to play in that memorable match.

Having beaten Scotland 4-3 at Hampden Park, and also Yugoslavia (2-0) at Wembley, England went on a short Scandinavian tour before the World Cup Finals began. The first game produced another clean sheet for goalkeeper Banks, as the tourists overcame Finland 3-0, and this was followed by a 6-1 victory over Norway, in which Jimmy Greaves netted four times, before Denmark were beaten 2-0. This was all very encouraging, and there was further encouragement in the shape of a 1-0 victory over Poland in Chorzow on 5 July. Just six days later, the real work began.

England were drawn in Group One

LEFT The Jules Rimet World Cup trophy

for the World Cup Finals, along with France, Mexico and Uruguay. A good start was important, and Alf Ramsey selected the following side for the opening game against Uruguay, at Wembley, on 4 July:

Gordon Banks, the Leicester City 'keeper who had by now made the England Number 1 shirt his own.

George Cohen, the Fulham right-back who, because of his tremendous speed, was a natural choice for Ramsey's 'wingless wonders'.

Ray Wilson, Everton's hard-tackling, constructive and reliable left back.

Nobby Stiles, the Manchester United wing-half with the toothy grin and indomitable spirit: the hard man of the side.

Jackie Charlton, the Leeds United centre-half, known to many as the 'giraffe'.

Bobby Moore, the cultured central defender from West Ham, who was the team captain.

Alan Ball, the Blackpool midfield player with tremendous energy.

Roger Hunt, the Liverpool inside-forward with excellent shooting skills.

John Connelly, an outside-right from Manchester United.

Jimmy Greaves, the inside-forward from Tottenham Hotspur, who was the most prolific goalscorer of his time.

Bobby Charlton of Manchester United, younger brother of Jackie

and another forward with exceptional shooting power.

More than 87,000 people witnessed a 0-0 draw and, although England were still very much in the World Cup, this was not the most auspicious of beginnings.

Ramsey made two changes for the game against Mexico, Ball and Connelly making way for Terry Paine, the speedy,

ABOVE The England
Team pose with the
Jules Rimet Trophy
after winning the
World Cup, 1966

two-footed Southampton winger, and
West Ham's Martin Peters, a midfielder
with outstanding talent and superb
passing skills. Undeterred by England's

failure to score against Uruguay, 92,570
souls turned up at Wembley. They
were lucky. Goals from Charlton and
Hunt secured a 2-0 victory, leaving only

France to be drawn with or beaten if England were to be sure of a place in the quarter-finals.

Wembley was almost full for the game against the French. Only one team change was made this time, Liverpool's Ian Callaghan coming in for Terry Paine. It seemed that Ramsey was having trouble accepting any kind of traditional winger in his side, and Callaghan was not to feature in the remaining three games. Roger Hunt was fast becoming the man of the tournament as far as England were concerned. The direct and resourceful '90-minute man' who had scored against Mexico now added another two against France. Banks once more kept a clean sheet – and England were in the quarter-finals.

Portugal, North Korea, the USSR, Hungary, West Germany, Uruguay and Argentina were the other quarter-finalists. There is almost always a surprise team in any tournament and this time it was North Korea, who had effectively knocked out mighty Italy in one of the most remarkable victories in World Cup history. Brazil failed to reach the last eight, star forward Pelé complaining bitterly about the lack of protection awarded him by referees.

England's quarter-final opponents were Argentina. Alan Ball came back into the side to replace Ian Callaghan, and there was one other change – Geoff Hurst, a third West Ham player, came in for Jimmy Greaves. It was, some said, a triumph of efficiency over genius.

The game against Argentina was not a pretty one to watch. At the end of a bruising 90 minutes which saw opposing captain Rattin sent off, many of the 90,584 people watching probably agreed with the sentiments expressed by the normally placid England manager who refused to let his players exchange shirts with their opponents after the match.

But England, thanks to Geoff Hurst's single goal, were in the semi-finals.

For the game against Portugal, Ramsey made no changes, even though Greaves was rumoured to be fully fit. Hurst had scored the only goal against Argentina and the manager saw no need to bring Greaves back.

The Portuguese side was undoubtedly one of the best in the World Cup Finals, even if the defence was at times a little suspect. Eusebio had netted four times in the 5-3 quarter-final defeat of North Korea, and he was to finish as the top scorer with nine strikes in all. His last goal came in the semi-final, as his side was to exit the competition with England's 2-1 victory. Portugal fought hard but could not overcome an inspired England side. More than 94,000 fans did their bit as well.

Bobby Charlton was to score both goals, and it was probably the finest game he played in an England shirt. After his second goal, several Portuguese players were moved to shake him by the hand – a fairly unusual event in such an important game. At the end of the 90 minutes, as the great Eusebio left the field in tears, Alf Ramsey permitted himself a rare smile. England had reached the Final of the World Cup.

West Germany had beaten the USSR 2-1 in their semi-final, with goals from Haller and Beckenbauer. Their team for the Final was: Hans Tilkowski, Horst-Dieter Hottges, Willi Schulz, Wolfgang Weber, Karl-Heinz Schnellinger, Franz Beckenbauer, Helmut Haller, Wolfgang Overath, Uwe Seeler, Siegfried Held and Lothar Emmerich. England's unchanged line-up consisted of Gordon Banks, George Cohen, Ray Wilson, Nobby Stiles, Jackie Charlton, Bobby Moore, Alan Ball, Martin Peters, Roger Hunt, Geoff Hurst and Bobby Charlton. Jimmy Greaves was most certainly fit by this time, but Ramsey again decided to stick with Hurst. Had things not gone England's way there can be no doubt that the press would have had a field day.

But things did go England's way – eventually. On the somewhat damp afternoon of Saturday 30 July 1966 the referee blew his whistle to signal the start of a football match which would never be forgotten by England supporters. The first half was not, however, very inspiring, and it all seemed to be going horribly wrong when, after just 12 minutes of play, Ray Wilson's error let in Helmut Haller.

Had Ramsey got it all wrong? Would his efficient and well organised side in the end prove less efficient and less well organised than the Germans? While these questions were no doubt going through the minds of those present, Hurst nodded home his captain's free kick to equalise.

Bobby Charlton was being shackled by central defender Franz Beckenbauer and, even though Martin Peters was having a great game, for a time the teams were locked in a kind of stale-

LEFT Alf Ramsey holds a Royal Brierley crystal football inscribed with the names of the 1966 World Cup winners

mate reminiscent of the First World War. Half-time came and went, and the game, along with the weather, began to improve. Then, after 77 minutes Peters, whom his manager had described as being "ten years ahead of his time", latched onto the ball following a blocked Hurst shot and put England ahead.

The English side had only to hold on for less than a quarter of an hour, and time was running out for the Germans who began piling in long-range shots from every angle and distance. With little more than seconds to go, a goalmouth mêlée, following a hotly-disputed free kick, ended up with Weber bundling the ball home. It looked as though Schnellinger had handled in the build-up, but if the Russian linesman missed it he was later to be forgiven.

The World Cup had been within England's grasp, but now the match was going into extra time. Ramsey raised morale by insisting to his players that they had beaten the Germans once, and now they had to do it again.

Next on the agenda was the most famous (or infamous, if you happen to be German) incident in World Cup football. A shot from Hurst hit

the underside of the bar, and came down on, or just behind, the goal-line. The film has been analysed by 'experts' time and again, but no firm conclusion has been reached. The balance of probability suggests that the whole of the ball did not in fact cross the line, but Geoff Hurst thought it did and, more importantly, so did the Russian linesman.

At the end, with West Germany pushing everyone forward in a last-ditch attempt to score another equaliser, Hurst again broke free. Some people were on the pitch, thinking it was all over – and it soon was. Hurst scored, the referee blew his whistle to signal the game's end, and England really had won the World Cup.

Ramsey next had to ensure qualification for the 1968 European Nations Cup, now re-named the European Championship. It was decreed that the Home Championship should double as the qualifying competition for British sides, and England's first game was at Windsor Park, Belfast, in October – a little under three months after the World Cup Final. Sir Alf (as he now was) probably felt obliged to field his World Cup-

winning team against Northern Ireland, and he did. They won 2-0, with goals from Hunt and Peters.

The same line-up was again employed against Wales in November, England winning 5-1 with goals from Hurst (2), both Charlton brothers and a Welsh defender. Some new players were introduced as the months went by, but for the game against Scotland at Wembley in April 1967 the only change from the World Cup-winning team was

February 1968, but they beat Wales and Northern Ireland again, and thus qualified for the European Championship quarter-finals.

The ties were played on a two-legged basis, and England were drawn against Spain. The England team for the first game, at Wembley on 3 April, was: Banks, Knowles, Wilson, Mullery, Jackie Charlton, Moore, Ball, Peters, Summerbee, Hunt and Bobby Charlton. England beat Spain by a goal to nil in the first encounter at Wembley, Bobby Charlton doing the damage. There were fears that a single goal was not enough, but those were to prove unfounded as, a month later, England ran out 2-1 winners with goals from Martin Peters and Norman Hunter. A hard-tackling defender, Hunter had replaced Summerbee in the line-up. Brian Labone, a centre-half who had, a few years earlier, joined Everton rather than go to university, had replaced Jackie Charlton, while Keith Newton, a cultured full-back from Blackburn Rovers, was in for Cyril Knowles.

that Greaves came in for Hunt. Jackie Charlton and Hurst scored for England, but Scotland gained a famous victory by three goals to two.

England were to earn a 1-1 draw in the return fixture with Scotland in

England had reached the semi-finals. They played a couple of friendlies, beating Sweden 3-1 and losing to West Germany (was that really a friendly?)

1-0, before they faced Yugoslavia, in Florence, on 5 June. It was a thoroughly bad-tempered affair and Alan Mullery became the first England player ever to be sent off. The World Champions were eventually beaten by a goal to nil, and were out of the European Championship.

The World Cup loomed once more, with the Finals to be played in Mexico. Altitude was always going to be a problem for the European sides but Sir Alf, together with the entire population of England, was confident that his team would do well. Substitutes were to be allowed for the first time in the World Cup, and red and yellow cards were also to be employed.

England's first group game was against Romania, and a Geoff Hurst goal was enough to win it. Five days later, Brazil were the opponents, and they proved to be just a little more difficult. The England side did well, but not quite well enough. Bobby Moore played superbly and Gordon Banks made one of the greatest saves in the history of the game when he leapt across his goal to save a header from Pele. In the end, however, it was all to no avail. Jeff Astle missed a relatively easy chance to equalise, and England lost 1-0.

England were, however, not yet out of it. A 1-0 win over Czechoslovakia, with Allan Clarke (who had played in place of Hurst) scoring from the spot, meant that they qualified for the quarter-finals against West Germany. It was to be revenge time for the Germans. Gordon Banks was, apparently, ill and was replaced in goal by Peter Bonetti. Bonetti was an excellent 'keeper, but this was not to be his day, and ever since he has been blamed for two of the goals which knocked England out of the competition.

All went wonderfully at first. England had gone two up, with goals from Mullery and Peters, but the team was visibly tiring as the game progressed. After 68 minutes, a routine shot from Franz Beckenbauer easily beat Bonetti, who went down too late. Eight minutes later, Uwe Seeler headed over the stranded England 'keeper, who this time had come off his line. The game went into extra time, during which Hurst had a 'goal' disallowed, and then Gerd Muller scored what proved to be the winner.

The dream had faded.

For Sir Alf, the writing was now on the dressing-room wall. Even so, his side took part in the 1972 European Championship Finals, after heading a qualifying group containing Switzerland, Greece and Malta. It was quarter-final time again, and West Germany were to exact further revenge. The match was played over two legs, the first being at Wembley. Germany scored first but Francis Lee equalised after 77 minutes, only for the Germans to score two late goals to put the tie beyond England's reach. The return leg in Berlin was scoreless, and England were out once more.

The end came for Sir Alf when England failed to qualify for the 1974 World Cup Finals. They had many chances to beat Poland in the last qualifying game, but in the end could only manage a 1-1 draw. By this time, Ramsey's tactics were considered to be out of date. The 'total football' played by Germany and Holland was proving far more effective, and thus Sir Alf was sacked shortly after the Poland game. Many felt that he had been badly treated as his teams had won 69 out of 113 internationals, losing only 17.

And he had won the World Cup.

Chapter 5

Total Football

NO-ONE KNOWS WHICH WORKER it was who took a football out of the British Isles for the first time and opened up the game overseas but the pace of development around the world was swift. By the turn of the twentieth century, the game was being played in almost every country. So much so that in 1903 talk first turned to setting up a world body to look after the interests of the game.

FIFA (the Federation of International Football Associations) was formed in Paris on 21 May 1904 and comprised France, Holland, Belgium, Switzerland, Denmark, Sweden and Spain. Although invited, not one of the Home Countries was represented, an isolationist attitude that was to have far-reaching implications for years to come. Not least was the decision that FIFA alone would have responsibility for establishing an international competition – the World Cup.

It took a further 26 years before the World Cup came into being but, as football grew in popularity around the world there was talk of club competitions involving the best European sides. However, the time teams would have to spend travelling to and from these countries made the idea of club competition impractical. All that was to change after World War II. Thanks to the development of air travel it was now possible to reach almost any part of Europe the same day. Equally, with floodlighting allowing evening matches, these would not interfere with work.

Three football matches proved the catalyst to establishing European competition. Two were the England side's disastrous performances against Hungary in 1953-54, while the third came in December 1954 when Wolves (then one of the leading club sides) exacted a revenge of sorts by beating Honved 3-2 in a friendly at Molineux.

According to the newspaper reports the following day, Wolves were now the greatest club side in Europe. While it may have been an audacious claim, it did at least galvanise French newspaper L'Equipe into inviting

BELOW Action from the Wolves v Honved match in 1954

TOTAL FOOTBALL

RIGHT Bertie Mee, the
manager of Arsenal
football club, with
the Fairs Cup which
the team won after
beating Anderlecht 3-0
at Highbury, 1970

what they regarded as the top 18 clubs in Europe to a meeting to discuss the formation of a European cup competition.

English Champions Chelsea were one of the 16 clubs that attended the meeting and, on 8 May 1955, the European Champion Clubs Cup came into being. Chelsea did not kick a single ball in anger, for the Football League asked them to reconsider their involvement lest their participation should lead to a fixture crisis. Hibernian (who weren't even Scottish Champions at the time, but were rated by L'Equipe as a better side than Aberdeen!) ended up £25,000 in profit after their European adventure.

The first Final, held in Paris, featured French Champions Stade De Reims and Spanish giants Real Madrid. Real were behind for only five minutes and then took the lead for the first time on 79 minutes. They held on to be crowned European Champions – it was to be a further five years before they lost the title.

While the European Champion Clubs Cup got off to a majestic start, the same could not be said for the Inter Cities Fairs Cup, also launched in 1955.

Twelve sides were invited to take part (invitations were extended to those cities which staged major trade fairs), but it took three years to get through the group stages, with both English entries (a composite London side and Birmingham City) advancing to the semi-finals.

Barcelona beat Birmingham and then beat London 8-2 on aggregate. Unlike the European Cup (as the premier club competition became known), the Fairs Cup was not a success, with the

23 games only producing a £3,500 profit after expenses – divided among the 12 competitors!

Real Madrid's victory in the European Cup had not gone unnoticed in England, where Manchester United had won the League and had every intention of competing in Europe in the 1956-57 season. Their adventure began in Belgium where they beat Anderlecht 2-0. The return was held at Maine Road (Old Trafford did not yet have floodlights) and more than 40,000

were treated to a magical display as United trounced Anderlecht 10-0. It was a little tighter in the next round, a 3-2 win over Borussia Dortmund at Maine Road being followed by a goalless draw in Germany.

Then it was off to Bilbao to meet Spanish Champions Atletico. After a 5-3 defeat United made up the deficit at Maine Road, winning 3-0 on the night. Their reward was a return to Spain to face holders Real, but with United on their way to another League title and the FA Cup Final, talk around Manchester was of a possible treble.

In the event this would have to wait more than four decades, for Real had a little too much experience for United, winning 3-1 in Madrid and drawing 2-2 at Old Trafford (floodlights having now been installed). Real were fortunate enough to host the Final in 1957, 124,000 of their fans seeing them triumph 2-0 over Italian side Fiorentina.

While United's treble dream died against Madrid (and even the Double eluded them as Aston Villa won the FA Cup Final), they did win the League and thus get another tilt at the European Cup. They faced Red Star Belgrade in the quarter-finals but won the home leg 2-1

IN MEMORY OF THE OFFICIALS & PLAYERS WHO LOST THEIR LIVES

WALTER CRICKMER   TOM CURRY

BERT WHALLEY

ROGER | BYRNE

GEOFF BENT   MARK JONES

EDDIE COLMAN   DAVID PEGG

DUNCAN EDWARDS   TOMMY TAYLOR

BILLY | WHELAN

IN THE MUNICH AIR DISASTER ON THE 6TH FEBRUARY 1958

aborted take offs; after the second one, the players returned to the waiting room and made phone calls.

At just after 3.00pm on 6 February the pilot was given permission to depart. This time the plane smashed into a house at the end of the runway, killing 23 passengers. Among the dead were eight of United's first team. Also dead were United's trainer, coach and secretary and eight journalists.

The whole of the footballing world was plunged into mourning for the great United side. In addition to those who died, both Jackie Blanchflower and Johnny Berry's injuries meant they never played again, and it was to take the recovering Matt Busby ten years to build another side capable of winning the European Cup.

A patched-up United beat AC Milan 2-1 at Old Trafford in the semi-final first leg thanks mainly to emotion but were cruelly exposed in the return as Milan won 4-0. But even Milan could not get the better of Real Madrid, who won 3-2 after extra time in Brussels. Real were able to extend their grip on the European Cup to five years after beating Stade De Reims in 1959 and then a year later seeing off Eintracht Frankfurt 7-3

and had a number of scares in the return on 5 February 1958 as they drew 3-3. On the way home, however, the plane stopped at snowbound Munich airport to refuel. It was still snowing as the plane attempted to take off and there were two

in a match that has since been regarded as one of the greatest club fixtures ever played.

Real's reign came to an end the following season when, for the first time in five years and after 20 ties, they lost 4-3 on aggregate to fellow Spanish side Barcelona in the first round. Barcelona made it to the Final that year, but any thought of the Cup remaining in Spain disappeared against Benfica, victors by three goals to two.

Benfica retained the trophy the following season, beating an over-the-hill Real Madrid 5-3 in Amsterdam. England's Spurs had emulated United's previous achievements by reaching the semi-final, but would have their moment of glory in the Cup Winners' Cup.

The success of the European Cup and a revised Inter Cities Fairs Cup had prompted calls for an additional European competition for national cup winners. This had been launched in 1960-61 and Rangers had made the Final before being beaten over two legs by Fiorentina. The Italian side reached the Final again before being beaten by Atletico Madrid after a replay.

Atletico also made the Final the following year when Jimmy Greaves and John White put Spurs 2-0 ahead by half-time. A penalty brought Atletico back into the game and for twenty minutes they laid siege to the Spurs goal, but the defence held firm – then two goals from Terry Dyson and another from Greaves earned Spurs the Cup 5-1.

Benfica's ending of Real Madrid's reign in the European Cup was to be followed by three years of Italian success. While Benfica and Real had been confident that they could score more goals than their opponents, AC and Inter were happy to score one

over Ferencvaros was followed by a 1-0 defeat, and, since UEFA had not yet implemented the away goals rule, a third, deciding game was won 2-1 by the Hungarians. They then beat Juventus on their home ground to become the first Eastern Bloc side to win a European trophy.

United were back in the European Cup the following season and reached the semi-finals once again. A dazzling performance against Benfica, with George Best running rings around their opponents (United won 5-1 in Lisbon), had convinced Busby that this might be their year. When they avoided

and shut up shop with the so-called catenaccio defence.

There was to be British success in Europe, however, for West Ham returned to Wembley in 1965 to lift the Cup Winners' Cup. Injuries left manager Ron Greenwood with the untried Alan Sealey as his attacking option in the Final against German side Munich 1860, but Sealey scored two goals in as many minutes to ensure West Ham's success.

The Inter-Cities Fairs Cup was still proving problematic, especially in the 1964-65 season. There were 48 entries, but with no byes in the first round two of six teams left in the quarter-finals got byes into the semis! They were to be joined by Manchester United, enjoying their best European run since the tragedy of 1958. A 3-2 home win

Real Madrid in the semi-finals and drew Partizan Belgrade, the stage was seemingly set for a romantic Final. It was not to be, however, for although United reduced a 2-0 deficit in the second, they could not get a further goal to level the aggregate score.

In the Final, Real secured their sixth European Cup with a 2-1 victory, Francisco Gento having appeared in all six victories and two losing Finals for good measure.

British sides had stumbled at the semi-final stage six times before finally going one step further in 1966-67. It was not to be Liverpool, England's entry, who were annihilated 7-3 on aggregate in the second round, but Jock Stein's Celtic. Inter Milan scored first in the Final and then closed down the game, seemingly having done enough to win the trophy. But Celtic's never-say-die attitude was to have the last laugh, with goals from Tommy Gemmell and Steve Chalmers cementing the reputation of manager Stein.

Celtic's defence of the trophy didn't get beyond the first round in 1967-68 but in what was the tenth anniversary of the Munich tragedy, there could be only one win-

ner – Manchester United. Their glory bid so nearly came off the rails in the semi-final against Real Madrid, for a 1-0 home victory was followed by a disastrous first half in the return that saw them 3-1 down and completely outplayed. Matt Busby threw caution to the wind in the second half, and goals from David Sadler and Munich survivor Bill Foulkes took them to the Final at Wembley.

There they faced Benfica, complete with Eusebio, Torres and other key Portuguese names. Bobby Charlton gave United the lead, only for Benfica to equalise with 15 minutes remaining. Eusebio might have wrapped it up with barely seconds to go when he burst through the United defence and had only Alex Stepney to beat but, in going for glory and blasting the ball as hard as he could, he hit it too close to Stepney and

BELOW A close-up of the new European Cup. Its purchase was necessary because Ajax retained the old one, having won it three times in succession

a point-blank save kept United in the game.

Their exertions in the 90 minutes had tired Benfica and, with more space to be found, United took control and scored three times in extra time, through George Best (a 25-yard run), birthday boy Brian Kidd and a second from Bobby Charlton. Charlton collected the trophy that meant more than any other to Manchester United.

The euphoria surrounding United's victory has always overshadowed Leeds United's triumph in the Fairs Cup that season. Beaten finalists in 1966-67 against Dynamo Zagreb, Leeds had been methodical and clinical in their run to the following year's Final against Ferencvaros. A single strike from Mick Jones in a bad-tempered first leg at Elland Road was enough to earn Leeds their second trophy of the season – they also lifted the League Cup in an equally dour match against Arsenal at Wembley.

As luck would have it, the city of Manchester

had two entries into the European Cup in 1968-69, Manchester City having won the League title. City would terrify Europe, according to co-manager Malcolm Allison, but they flopped in the first round at Fenerbahce. United meanwhile made it to the semi-final but couldn't overcome AC Milan to make the Final a perfect swansong for their manager. It was to be another United, Newcastle, who triumphed in Europe, winning the Fairs Cup after overcoming Ujpest Dozsa. Manchester City got revenge of sorts by lifting the European Cup Winners' Cup in 1970. Arsenal won the Fairs Cup, while Celtic lost in the European Cup Final to Dutch Champions Feyenoord.

While English sides may have dominated the Fairs Cup/UEFA Cup and even the Cup Winners' Cup (Manchester City's success in 1970 being followed by a replay victory for Chelsea over Real Madrid a year later), Dutch football was in the ascendant. Feyenoord's success came as a surprise, not least because they were not even rated the best side in Holland. That honour fell to the Johann Cruyff-inspired Ajax, who confirmed their reputation with a hat-trick of European

LEFT Dutch
midfielder Johann
Cruyff, 1974

have far to travel, either, Rangers beating Moscow Dynamo 3-2 after being 3-0 up inside 50 minutes. Their good work was undone by their supporters, however, who fought bitter battles with the Spanish police (the match was played in Barcelona).

There was more trouble the following year, with Leeds this time the victims of a Greek referee and an Italian keeper. AC Milan's Vecchi gave the performance of his career to keep out shot after shot, but he was aided by some curious decisions from Greek referee Christos Michas, denying Leeds two blatant penalties.

Liverpool finally got a winning streak going in the UEFA Cup, seeing off holders Spurs in the semi-final and then beating Borussia Moenchengladbach in the Final 3-2 on aggregate to complete an unique double – they also won the League title.

Borussia's passage to the Final showed that it was Germany's turn to dominate Europe, and after Ajax's triple success in the European Cup came three successes for Bayern Munich. The first of these was achieved after a replay against Atletico Madrid, a 1-1 draw being followed two days later by

Cups in 1971-73 thanks to Cruyff, Neeskens and Muhren.

In contrast, Leeds were still methodical and clinical in equal measure, winning the Fairs Cup on away goals after a 2-2 draw in Turin against Juventus and 1-1 at Elland Road. That was the last Fairs Cup Final, for the following season the UEFA Cup was launched, Tottenham and Wolves contesting the Final. Spurs won 3-2 on aggregate. Scotland ensured the European Cup Winners' Cup didn't

a 4-0 hammering. The 1973-74 season, however, was completely overshadowed by crowd violence at Feyenoord, where England's run in the UEFA Cup came to an end with Tottenham's 2-0 defeat.

Liverpool repeated their 1972-73 double in 1975-76, winning the League title from QPR and beating Bruges in the Final of the UEFA Cup. Bob Paisley's side spent the following year (1976-77) pursuing a treble of League, FA Cup

and European Cup, it was only the FA Cup that let the club down, Manchester United winning at Wembley. The European Cup was the real prize, and in Rome against Borussia Moenchengladbach they powered their way to a 3-1 victory.

Liverpool retained the trophy the following year, a single strike from Kenny Dalglish at Wembley enough to beat FC Bruges (Liverpool's first four

European victories were achieved against the same two sides). Then the mantle passed to Brian Clough's Nottingham Forest, surprise League Champions in 1977-78.

A 3-3 draw at the City Ground in the semi-final convinced Cologne they were destined for the Final, but an Ian Bowyer goal was enough to earn Forest a Final appearance in Munich. There Clough played his talisman, £1 million Trevor Francis, who scored the only goal of the game against Malmo. Forest retained the trophy the following year in yet more

emphatic style. The Final against SV Hamburg (with former Liverpool hero Kevin Keegan) was another single-goal victory, the hero John Robertson.

The 1980-81 European Cup Final pitted Real Madrid, in their first Final since 1966, against Liverpool, Alan Kennedy scoring the only goal. In an era when winning was all that mattered, Liverpool were to prove the English were better at it than anyone else, as Ipswich Town, victors in the UEFA Cup that same season, confirmed.

If Forest were Europe's surprise package, few could account for how Aston Villa triumphed in 1981-82. They overcame a number of mishaps along the way, not least in the Final

ABOVE Aston Villa players celebrate victory after the European Cup Final against Bayern Munich, May 1982

LEFT Trevor Francis celebrates scoring the winning goal by lifting the European Cup after the Final between Nottingham Forest and Malmo, 1979

TOTAL FOOTBALL

BELOW The barriers collapse as supporters try to get on to the pitch during the European Cup Final between Liverpool and Juventus at the Heysel Stadium

against Bayern Munich when after eight minutes veteran goalkeeper Jimmy Rimmer was injured. Nigel Spink, who had played only one game prior to that night, let nothing in, while at the other end Peter Withe scored off the post to collect England's sixth European Cup win on the trot.

If 1982-83 was barren for the English, then the Scots had much to cheer. The Old Firm duopoly of Celtic and Rangers had been broken by the new firm of Dundee United and Aberdeen, with the former winning the League title and the latter retaining their Scottish Cup and also winning in Europe. Their Final vic-

tory over Real Madrid in the European Cup Winners' Cup was achieved after extra time, vindicating Alex Ferguson's rigorous training regime.

Liverpool and Spurs triumphed after penalty shoot-outs in the European Cup and UEFA Cup respectively in 1983-84. If Spurs were fortunate winners (it was generally agreed that Anderlecht were slightly the better of the two sides over the two legs), then the same could not be said for Liverpool, who faced Roma on their home ground. Phil Neal gave them the lead, only for Pruzzo to equalise, and with no more goals the stage was set for another penalty shootout.

While the UEFA Cup had made a hero out of Spurs keeper Tony Parks, so the European Cup Final made the reputation of Liverpool's Bruce Grobbelaar, whose antics forced Conti and Graziani to blast over the top. Alan Kennedy's vital strike secured a unique treble of League title, League Cup and European Cup in new manager Joe Fagan's debut season.

The only trophy to elude Liverpool that year was the FA Cup, won by fellow Merseysiders Everton. The following season saw Everton emerge as the

new force in English football, snatching the League from their closest rivals, reaching the FA Cup Final and winning the European Cup Winners' Cup, beating Rapid Vienna.

How good Everton were or could have been will never be known, for English fans' already tarnished reputation was demolished for good on 29 May 1985. With the domestic game already reeling from the events of the Bradford fire 18 days earlier, which had claimed 56 lives, the last thing England needed was trouble on the European front. Unfortunately, the European showpiece between Liverpool

ABOVE The European dream goes sour for a Liverpool fan. The club's post-Heysel ban hit them and English football hard

and Juventus at the Heysel Stadium in Brussels saw trouble before, during and after the match, left 39 dead and resulted in English clubs being banned from European competition indefinitely.

The game itself, which was only played because the authorities feared further rioting should they abandon it, was won 1-0 by Juventus via

a hotly disputed penalty (the tragedy has always overshadowed Juve's accomplishment of becoming the first side to win all three European trophies on offer, following their victories in the UEFA Cup in 1977 and the Cup Winners' Cup in 1984). England's period of domination was at an end.

And how. In the 30 or so years of European competition prior to Heysel, English sides had won the European Cup eight times, the European Cup Winners' Cup five times and the UEFA Cup eight times for a total of 21 European victories, more than any other country. More importantly, the victories were spread around 12 clubs, reflecting the strength in depth of the English game.

No-one really took over after English clubs were banned. If anything, the European game suffered as much as the English game from the ban; English clubs had understood the mechanics of cup competition, perhaps better than their rivals. Few would have approached the European Cup Final in 1986 as did Steaua Bucharest, who showed no sign of wanting to beat Barcelona

RIGHT
Demetrio Albertini
(front) of AC Milan
keeps possession
of the ball from a
Barcelona player
during the European
Cup
Final, 1994

in 120 minutes, preferring the lottery of a penalty shootout. In a match Terry Venables' side should have won, they lost 2-0 on penalties.

It was not until 1990 that a club side managed to retain the European Cup again, AC Milan's four-goal hammering of Steaua in 1989 followed by a 1-0 victory over a resurgent Benfica in 1990. The following year it was back to the penalty shootout, Red Star Belgrade winning 5-3 against Marseille after 120 minutes had produced no goals and little entertainment.

That same season (1990-91) had finally seen English clubs re-admitted to European competition, Manchester United making up for lost time with a victory in the Cup Winners' Cup against Barcelona. It was manager Alex Ferguson's second victory in the competition, following Aberdeen's triumph in 1983, and striker Mark Hughes; considered a flop at Barcelona, scored both goals in United's 2-1 win against his former club.

Barcelona had more to cheer the following season, finally winning the European Cup at the third time of asking. Beating Sampdoria at Wembley after extra time, Barca emulated Juventus' achievement of having won all three European trophies.

As noted earlier, it was the French who had been largely responsible for the creation of the European Cup back in 1955, but the champagne was to remain on ice for 38 years. In 1993, Marseille, making their second Final appearance, finally got their hands on the trophy, beating AC Milan 1-0. They were to be subsequently stripped of the title, however, after it was revealed they had bribed an opposition team in the run-up to winning the French title a year before.

AC Milan were back the following year, hammering Barcelona 4-0 in Athens to register their fifth European Cup win, while in the Cup Winners' Cup Arsenal added their second European trophy (after the 1970 Fairs Cup). The Final against Parma ended "1-0 to the Arsenal", as their fans would sing, thanks to Alan Smith.

There were new plans for the European Cup, however. Since its formation in 1955 it had always been played as a straight knockout competition, the aggregate winner advancing to the next stage. The bigger clubs in Europe, in particular the Italian

and Spanish, wanted guarantees of more games, together with the match and television income it would generate.

UEFA finally capitulated, announcing that from 1994-95 the European Cup would be replaced by the UEFA Champions League. Preliminary rounds produced 16 sides who would compete in four mini leagues, guaranteeing each side six games in the first round. The top two in each table advanced to the quarter-finals, where the competition reverted to a knockout format. Group D produced both finalists, Ajax beating AC Milan 1-0 in the Final having already

beaten them home and away in the group stages.

The new competition, with its subsequent amendment of a second round of group matches, has achieved what the big clubs wanted; extra matches that produced extra revenue. Real Madrid were widely reported to be the richest club in Europe, and the money generated by all these extra games was invested in the acquisition of new players, often the best the world had to offer.

In between Real's domination of the Champions League, there have been victories other clubs can savour. Chief among these would be Manchester United's win over Bayern Munich in 1999, which enabled them to complete the ultimate treble of FA Premiership, FA Cup and European Cup. Bayern took the lead in the Final through Basler and the clocks showed time up when United won a corner. Goalkeeper Schmeichel ran the length of the pitch to join this last-ditch attempt at an equaliser, and in the ensuing confusion Teddy Sheringham fired home from short range.

Extra time looked assured when United won another corner; this time, Sheringham's flick was met by Solskjaer and they had

grabbed victory from the jaws of defeat. Fittingly, it would have been Sir Matt Busby's 90th birthday on the day, 26 May 1999. Like Busby, United manager Alex Ferguson was rewarded with a knighthood, a fitting award for one of the most successful European managers of the modern era.

Bayern would bounce back in 2001, winning on penalties against Valencia, while earlier there had been another German triumph, with Borussia Dortmund beating Juventus 3-1 in 1997. Unfancied Leverkusen might have made it a German hat-trick in 2002, but in the space of a little over a week they lost the German Championship, the German League and UEFA Champions League, going down to Real Madrid 2-1 in the Final of the latter.

While there have been lots of extra games for Europe's elite thanks to the new formats, it has been at the expense of everyone else. The European Cup Winners' Cup was scrapped in 1999, Lazio becoming the last ever holders

LEFT Manchester United manager Alex Ferguson is held aloft by Wes Brown (left) and Raimond van der Gouw as they celebrate victory in the European Champions League Final, 1999

by beating Mallorca 2-1 in the Final at Villa Park. Arsenal might have retained the cup in 1995 but were beaten by an audacious lob from Nayim in the last minute of extra time against Zaragoza, while Chelsea restored English pride with victory in 1998 over Stuttgart.

The format of the UEFA Cup has been redesigned, as the survivors are now joined midway through the competition by the unsuccessful sides from the Champions League. Thus Arsenal started the 1999-2000 season in the Champions League and ended it in the UEFA Cup Final (they lost on penalties). Even the Final is now a single-match affair, complete with sudden death or golden goal endings, which saw Liverpool claim their third UEFA Cup in 2001. A 'silver goal' system was introduced in 2003 and came into immediate effect as Porto beat Celtic 3-2 after extra time to win the Final.

Liverpool and Chelsea played a two-legged semi-final in April 2005 to decide who would have the right to face AC Milan in the Final. Liverpool, who won the encounter, had played Juventus in the previous round for the first time since Heysel: many expressions of regret and remembrance were made,

including a ceremony involving past players, but not all Juventus fans were prepared to forgive and forget.

It was Milan's second Final in three years and they were bookies' favourites to win – but Liverpool overturned the odds in improbable fashion. Three goals down at half-time, they fought back to equalise on the hour and, with no further score, eventually triumphed on penalties in what the press were calling the greatest Champions League Final ever.

Arsenal were England's representatives the following year, but failed to make their first Final appearance a successful one, Barcelona coming from behind to win 2-1.

Liverpool were back in the Final in 2007 where Milan gained revenge for their defeat two years earlier – winning 2-1 at the Olympic Stadium in Athens.

The 2008 Final was uniquely contested by two English teams, arch rivals Manchester United and Chelsea. Played in Moscow, it was a closely fought affair that went to penalties after extra time. Chelsea's centre-forward Didier Drogba had let down the team by stupidly getting sent off for retaliation; so it was up to skipper John Terry to step into the

breach and take his penalty. He only needed to score to bring the Cup back to The Bridge for the first time but he slipped in his run-up and his scuffed shot grazed the outside of the post. Manchester United secured the trophy after keeper Van der Sar had saved a weak Nicolas Anelka spot kick; and they were back in the Final the following year when they lost to Barcelona –the fourth year in a row, though, that an English team had been in the Final.

England's dominance of the competition was finally ended when Internazionale (managed by Jose Mourinho) won a tactical battle against Bayern Munich in 2010; although Manchester United were back the following year when they were comprehensively outplayed by Barcelona.

While the crème de la crème were battling it out for the biggest club prize in the world, Europe's governing body had merged the UEFA Cup with the Intertoto Cup in the 2009-10 season to create the Europa League – a somewhat second rate competition that most top teams find a distraction to their heavily crowded seasons.

Indeed, fans are hard pressed to remember who has won this competi-

tion so far (Atletico Madrid have won it twice in 2010 and 2012) although the 2013 Final was given more of a degree of fascination as it was contested by Chelsea and Benfica – with the Blues winning in extra time and becoming the first-ever English team to win all three separate European cup competitions.

Meanwhile, the Champions League is seen by many of the top clubs as a more important competition than their own domestic leagues. Certainly, the German fans of Bayern Munich saw winning the final in Wembley 2013 as a bigger triumph than winning their own league which they had won at a canter against mostly meagre opposition.

The time will soon come when the top European clubs turn their backs on their own national leagues and start to contest a European Super League – which will produce the biggest games, the biggest television audiences and the biggest money.

ABOVE Liverpool players hold up the Champions League trophy to the thousands of fans gathered to welcome them home following their victory over AC Milan, 2005

Chapter 6

Premier Passions

THE PREMIER LEAGUE, FOUNDED in 1992, effectively represented a breakaway from the Football League by its top clubs. With the League a semi-democratic organisation, the bigger clubs felt their smaller brethren were dictating the way the game was run and how the finances were being distributed.

The Football League, formed in 1888 with an initial membership of 12, had, by the late 1980s, grown to 92 clubs. Yet this had been by a process of evolution, rather than revolution.

By 1919 the First Division had reached a figure of 22 clubs, a membership it was to retain until 1987. The Second Division's growth kept similar pace, while the introduction of a Third Division in 1920 (enlarged and split into North and South in 1921) had

brought the League's strength up to 86 clubs. By 1950 the membership stood at 92, the figure it would retain for four decades.

When the war in Europe ended and the Football League resumed, more than 157 million people passed through the turnstiles in the first four years of League football.

A more interesting figure was revealed at the end of the 1947-48 season when the BBC claimed more than one million had witnessed the FA Cup Final between Manchester United and Blackpool on TV. Although television had existed before the war, there were insufficient numbers of sets to unduly worry football; after the war the tide turned.

It was not until 1966 that television was blamed for adversely affecting a

gate; on 5 May that year, the live broadcast of the European Cup Winners' Cup Final between Liverpool and Borussia Dortmund was specifically mentioned as a reason why only 4,554 turned up at Highbury to watch Arsenal face Leeds United, second in the table at the time, in a First Division match. In 1982, the televising of the FA Cup Final replay between Spurs and QPR was similarly held to blame for only 2,315 attending the international between Wales and

ABOVE Arsenal team members peering into a camera after playing in the first football match to be shown live on television

Northern Ireland, the lowest figure to have witnessed an international fixture since 1892.

While live televised football was still some way off, football fans unable to get to games did at least start to get a regular fix of the game with the launch of BBC's Match Of The Day in August 1964. Hosted by Kenneth Wolstenholme, the opening show chose the Champions Liverpool's clash with Arsenal for its first main feature and was rewarded with a viewing figure of some 75,000, only slightly more than had witnessed the game live at Anfield.

Match Of The Day's viewing figures soon picked up and it became the football programme to watch on a Saturday night. Independent Television's version screened on a Sunday afternoon was never going to match it and ITV realised that the only way they were going to get similar viewing figures was in poaching the rights from the BBC. In November 1978 they believed they had done so. The BBC launched a court action and it was decided the two channels would alternate coverage from season to season during the course of a four-year deal. While the club chairmen had no wish to commit themselves to

such a long-term deal, football needed television far more than television needed football.

In 1983 the Football League accepted a £1 million a season sponsorship deal with the electrical manufacturers Canon for three years. At the same time, the bigger clubs won an important change in the rules with regard to gate receipts; all clubs now got to keep their home receipts rather than splitting the take with a percentage going to the League. It was estimated that Coventry City, as an example, would lose some £60,000 a year, but somehow the big guns prevailed.

While more and more outside money may have been coming into the game (the Milk Marketing Board now sponsored the League Cup) football itself suffered a nightmare decade during the 1980s. Most of the game's problems were caused by the fans themselves – rioting by Millwall fans at Luton during a Cup tie led to the home side banning away supporters altogether for a time, England fans were considered the scourge of Europe after smashing up shops and businesses in Luxembourg, and there were incidents at matches up and down the country.

RIGHT Fire damage at Bradford's Valley Parade where 56 fans died

Two disasters in particular would have a considerable effect on football, culminating in a complete change in the League's makeup. A fire in the main stand at Bradford City midway through their final League match of the season against Lincoln City on 11 May 1985 left 56 people dead. Eighteen days later the European Cup Final between Liverpool and Juventus saw some of the worst scenes ever witnessed as Liverpool fans charged their rivals and 39 spectators were crushed to death after a wall collapsed.

The repercussions were immense. As a result of the Bradford fire, new regulations were brought in that would effectively close or severely restrict the use of wooden stands. Many of the football stadiums in the country were approaching 100 years old, and many had structures similar to that which had gone up in flames at Valley Parade, Bradford. Football was going to be faced with a huge bill for rebuilding. UEFA's response to the Heysel disaster was to ban all English clubs from European competition indefinitely, and Liverpool for an extra three years beyond the (unspecified) date when English clubs were admitted back.

In January 1985 the clubs had rejected a £16 million four-year deal for the televising of League football, believing the television companies could afford and would pay more. They didn't, and the 1985-86 season kicked off with no television deal in place; when a deal was subsequently reached some months later, it was football that had its cap in its

would be needed to effect any change.

Renewed negotiations with the television companies were completed quickly, not least because football needed the income. A two-year agreement worth £6.2 million was reached in June, at much the same time it was announced that the First Division was to shrink to 20 clubs over the next two years. Play-offs, which had been a feature of the Football League when the Second Division kicked off in 1892, were to be re-introduced. For now, all talk of a breakaway Super League had been quietened.

The occasion of the Football League's centenary in 1988-89 should have been a cause for celebration. Unfortunately the season will forever be remembered for the tragic events of 15 April.

The FA Cup semi-final between Liverpool and Nottingham Forest at Hillsborough was a repeat of the previous year's clash. Since that earlier match had passed largely without incident, the authorities, both police and football, believed similar arrangements for the second match would suffice. As it was, fundamental errors made at the first match were repeated at the second, this time with

hand, settling for a mere £1.3 million for the rest of the season.

The First Division clubs began to get their own way in April 1986 when the voting structure of the Football League changed to reflect their influence – from now on the Second, Third and Fourth Divisions would have a smaller block vote, and only a two-thirds majority

PREMIER PASSIONS

BELOW Disaster strikes before the FA Cup semi-final match between Liverpool and Nottingham Forest at Hillsborough

catastrophic consequences.

Although Liverpool had an average attendance of 40,000, they were allocated 24,000 tickets for the semi-final, while Forest, with an average of 17,000, were allocated 30,000. Some ten minutes before kick-off, with more than three thousand Liverpool supporters still trying to gain admission to their allocated Leppings Lane End stand, the

police took the decision to open the gates. Perimeter fencing, designed to keep fans off the pitch, also had the effect of keeping trapped fans in place, and in the ensuing panic and crush 96 people were to lose their lives.

After decades of neglect and complacency, football's shortcomings were cruelly exposed. The game had ignored fans' requirements for decades, treating them all as potential hooligans and caging them in pens from which there was little or no escape. Matters at Hillsborough were made worse by poor communication between police and stewards and a lack of first aid and emergency medical equipment.

In truth, this was a disaster that could have happened at almost any ground in the country. Renovation and modernisation at many had only taken place when legislation (such as that introduced after the

LEFT Tributes cover
a fence and path in
the aftermath of the
Hillsborough disaster

Bradford fire) dictated. Football clubs had not been helped over the years by the tax laws. Spending profits on the acquisition of new players did not incur tax liability; improving facilities did. Little wonder grounds had been largely ignored for so many years.

The resulting enquiry into the disaster, which led to the publication of the Taylor Report, was to have far-reaching consequences for the game, not least the removal of all standing areas and a move towards all-seater stadiums. The cost to the game was going to be huge, and for once the cost could not be passed on directly to the supporters.

RIGHT Gordon Taylor, who became secretary of the Professional Football Association

Almost as soon as the report was published, so the clubs began to backtrack – how were the First Division clubs going to fund such enforced renovation when the game's finances were shrinking? What was needed was more games, so a plan to reduce the size of the First Division to 18 (and possibly even lower) was effectively rescinded. In August 1990, therefore, the clubs agreed to return to a 22-club top division.

That same month the clubs announced they were to sign a television deal with Sky and ITV, with 115 matches to be screened live during the course of the season. This caused bickering between the Football League and Football Association, both of whom believed they ran the game, and prompted a court case between the two organisations. The FA announced in April 1991 that it was to create an

18-team Super League, commencing in the 1992-93 season, further details of which were to be revealed in a forthcoming 'blueprint'. On 14 June, 16 First Division clubs signed a document indicating their intention to join: three did not vote and the remaining three voted against.

Five days later the FA released their 119-page Blueprint For The Future Of Football. Aside from the already well-publicised Premier League, which the FA would run, it also contained details of criteria which would have to met by any club wishing to gain promotion to the League – an all-seater stadium with a minimum capacity of 20,000. The Premier League would contain 22 clubs initially, reducing to 18 as soon as was practical, and the remaining 70 Football League clubs was split into new First, Second and Third Divisions, with 22 in the First Division and 24 in each of the other two.

Since the Premier League was to be financed largely by an influx of television money, there were concessions towards the armchair viewer: there would be live screening of a Premier League match every week, along with every England international. A little over a week later, 15 First Division clubs agreed to resign from the Football League.

The following day, a further five followed suit and, at the FA's summer meeting in Torquay, the remaining two clubs committed themselves to the cause, with newly-elected chairman and spokesman Rick Parry announcing the clubs would either follow the FA's plan or go it alone. The Football League as it had been for over a hundred years, was effectively history from that moment.

BELOW Rick Parry of the Premier League who went on to become Liverpool's chief executive

BELOW Television cameras in Italy

On 17 July 1991, the majority of First Division clubs signed a 'founder member document', binding them to the forthcoming Premier League.

Although the Second Division clubs had not been consulted over any aspect of the new competition, they were offered an olive branch with the promise of

three clubs to be promoted while the Premier League remained at 22 clubs.

The following day, the Football Association successfully applied to have the hearing of the Football League's £9 million damages claim delayed until a court could decide whether the FA's plans for the Premier League were legal.

With the new (and last in its traditional form) Football League season just days away, the game was in danger of imploding. A League management committee meeting ended in farce for, with four of the proposed Premier League clubs ineligible to vote, there weren't enough members to form a quorum! The Third and Fourth Division clubs, who had hardly a voice in any of the discussions, announced they would boycott the FA Cup if they felt their position was being undermined.

In an attempt at mediation, FA Secretary Graham Kelly offered the Football League the opportunity of coming under the FA umbrella and working side by side with the Premier League, an offer that was rejected (Kelly had been secretary to the Football League before taking up his position within the FA!).

Isolation was never a serious option, and the FA agreed to three up to and three down from the Premier League. The real cause of the bickering, however, was revealed in the Football League's cash demands from the Premier League; £6 million per year for 50 years by way of compensation! Eventually, after more than five months of wrangling, a compromise was reached, with the FA paying £2 million and the Premier League clubs £1 million for the next five years – £15 million as opposed to the £300 million the League had originally demanded.

The Premier League, with all the legal wrangles out of the way, officially came into being on 23 September 1991. The Football League's Rule 11, which had demanded three-year resignation notices from the clubs, was revoked by 51 votes to 9. The 22-club Premier League would also eventually reduce to 20, although there was no stipulation as to when this might occur.

The following month, on 10 October, the Premier League held its first meeting and set up a number of committees to formulate rules and a constitution. This seemed to take over a month and discussions were never fully revealed, but a five-page draft did confirm that there would definitely be

22 founder members, the reduction to 20 clubs being delayed until 1994-95.

While relations between the FA and Football League may have thawed, the Professional Footballers Association was proving a tougher nut to crack. Gordon Taylor threatened a players strike unless they were consulted more by the new League, and won backing from the members to hold such a strike unless the PFA were admitted to negotiations. A peace offer from the Premier League in March was rejected by Taylor, and a vote of all PFA members backed him by 548 votes to 37. Finally, on 27 April, the PFA accepted a £1.5 million offer from the Premier League.

As the final Football League season as was came to an end, with Leeds United taking the First Division title ahead of a Manchester United side that should have won it, we got a glimpse of the Premier League's promised land. On 18 May the FA signed a new television deal with satellite channel BSkyB and the BBC, collecting £304 million over five years in a deal that guaranteed 60 live matches a season (to be screened on a Sunday afternoon and Monday evening on BSkyB) and highlight programmes on Saturday evening and midweek (on the BBC).

More importantly for the clubs concerned, the television money would be split equally among those who had helped earn it, rather than distributed to all 92 clubs in the 'old-style' League. There would also be payments for staging televised matches, far in excess of the money that had been on offer under previous deals. Then clubs had merely been compensated for any shortfall in their crowd figures and income. (In 2003 Fulham collected almost £650,000 for the 'inconvenience' of playing two televised matches in three days.)

ITV launched a court bid to get the deal overturned, thus delaying the backslapping for a further month, but in the meantime secured their own deal with the Football League, paying a minimum of £25 million over four years for exclusive highlights of the League and (then Rumbelows-sponsored) League Cup and live screening of the latter's semi-finals and Final. There would also be a number of unspecified live matches.

LEFT
Roman Abramovich,
Chelsea's multi-
millionaire owner,
waves to supporters
at Stamford Bridge

While the clubs who were to form the new Premier League readied themselves for the forthcoming launch, the old Football League reinvented itself... by renaming the Second, Third and Fourth Divisions the new First, Second and Third! (The current names are Championship, League One and League Two.) Clubs would be rewarded for success on a sliding scale which borrowed its principle from the Premier League, and there was a return to the 'one club, one vote' rule that had held back the bigger clubs for almost a century.

The size of the Leagues did not alter much either, although Aldershot had been forced to resign during the 1991-92 campaign owing to financial difficulties, the first club to do so midway through a season since Accrington Stanley in 1961-62. Things wouldn't be noticeably different in the Premier League either, although there would now be three substitutes instead of two, a 15-minute half-time break and referees would wear green.

The 'new, improved' Premier League finally kicked off for most clubs on 15 August 1992, with Nottingham Forest and Liverpool meeting in the first Sunday televised game the following day

RIGHT Arsenal's
captain Thierry Henry
has a shot during
their Premiership
match against
Fulham at Highbury,
2005

and QPR and Manchester City clashing in the first Monday-night match a day later.

Although Leeds United had triumphed in the last 92-club Football League season, the ensuing 21 years saw Manchester United by far the most successful club both on and off the pitch winning the Premier League 13 times since its formation.

Their predominance was very much due to manager Sir Alex Ferguson who retired at the end of the 2013 season (to be replaced by David Moyes) after 27 years in charge proving to be their most successful supremo since the legendary Sir Matt Busby. His achievement of the treble of League, FA Cup and European Champions League success in 1998-99 season is unlikely to ever be eclipsed.

His longest-serving rival was the urbane Frenchman Arsene Wenger whose Arsenal side won the Premier League three times; while Chelsea, under different managers, won the league in 2005, 2006 and 2010. Incredibly, the league was won by Blackburn Rovers in 1995 who have since plummeted down the league and are now languishing in the lower half of the Championship.

United's dominance was also punc-

RIGHT Eric Cantona one of the first foreign players to play in the Premier League

tuated by their "noisy neighbours" Manchester City in 2012 when they won on goal difference on the last day of the season with Sergio Aguero scoring in extra time to beat QPR in the greatest finish the league will probably ever see.

The Scots had formed their own Premier Division as long ago as 1975 to increase the number of competitive games played by the top-flight teams. A Third Division was introduced in 1994, with all divisions being reduced to 10 in number, but the top teams broke away three years later, in emulation of those south of the border, to negotiate their own TV rights. Promotion and relegation to and from the (currently 12-strong) Scottish Premier League remained, albeit only one club a season and that subject to ground criteria.

The new division continued to be dominated by Celtic and Rangers, although the duopoly was broken when Rangers entered insolvency in 2012 and were liquidated. Rangers were re-launched by a new company and placed in the Third Division – rendering the Premier League a walk in the park for Celtic until Rangers get back to the big time.

If there has been one central theme

to the English Premier League since its inauguration then it is money. Prize money is offered to clubs on a sliding scale according to their League position at the end of the season. There are 'parachute' payments made to clubs who are relegated at the end of each season, but such are the potential riches that are on offer in the Premier League it has become a holy grail for virtually every Football League club.

As many have found out, reaching the Premier League is significantly easier than staying in it, and the number of clubs who have made an immediate return to the First Division after 12 months in the promised land continues to grow. There is little evidence that this trend will ever be reversed, for many clubs are finding that the cost of maintaining their Premier League status on Football League income makes for an impossible equation.

It is now said there are three mini-Leagues within the Premier League; a top table featuring the likes of Manchester United, Manchester City, Chelsea and Arsenal who have been rewarded for their consistency in the Premier League with the better part of the prize money on offer and additional income from campaigns in the UEFA Champions League their Premier League position has earned them. Then there is the middle table, at which sit the likes of Liverpool, Spurs and Everton who would like to join those at the top table but lack the consistency and therefore the funds to make that transition. They also cast cautious eyes over those on the bottom table, usually occupied by those coming up from the First Division and likely to make a speedy return.

Players' union boss Gordon Taylor may well have received continuing mandates to extract a larger share of the television money on offer, but it has been achieved at a high price to his members. As salaries and transfer fees escalated in the UK, many clubs began to look for cheaper alternatives and invariably found them in eastern Europe. With lower fees for players often of better ability than those on offer in the UK, the Premier League began to take on the look of the United Nations, players from as far afield as Australia, America, Lithuania, Estonia, the Czech Republic, Brazil, France, Nigeria, China and Japan plying their trade.

Another trend is the tendency towards club interests over those of the national

BELOW Ruud van Nistelrooy holds up a Manchester United scarf after signing for the club

teams. Club chairmen are not primarily interested in helping the national side, since it is they that pay the players their wages: this has led to continuing battles between the England manager and club bosses over the years. Thirty years ago, having a player picked to represent England (or any other country) was an honour; now it is an inconvenience. Yet the same club managers will happily pay transfer fees for players who regularly represent the likes of Japan, China and Brazil and require additional travelling time to and from international matches.

While the standard of football it is possible to watch in England has undoubtedly improved since the Premier League came into being with talents of the calibre of Ronaldo, Suarez and Mata on display, it has been achieved at a cost. At the time of the abolition of the maximum wage in the 1960s, it was widely held that, since being a footballer was such a short-term occupation, the players owed it to themselves to earn as much out of the game as they could in order to prepare for a life outside the game once their playing days were at an end. Now, it is claimed that even an average Premier League player only needs a single season's money in order to set himself up for life. Fans can only look on in disbelief as some players collect £250,000 a week for playing the game. Add to this income from sponsorship and endorsements and several players are earning more than £15 million every year. Little wonder more and more clubs are falling into debt. Unfortunately, as Leeds United found out to their cost in 2003, the bigger the ambition the bigger the bill, the bigger the headache the bigger the pill. While, for a few, the Premier League has been an unqualified success, for the rest it remains an expensive exercise.

LEFT Patrick Vieira, a very successful import for Arsenal, lifts the Championship trophy, 1998

Chapter 7

Football
Goes Global

FOOTBALL IN THE TWENTY-FIRST century is a truly global game, thanks to the advance of satellite communications. It's a situation FIFA (Federation Internationale de Football Association, the world governing football body) has sought to foster in recent years by staging the World Cup in new territories.

The first tournament of the current millennium was jointly hosted for the first time by two countries, Japan and South Korea. It followed in the footsteps of the United States eight years earlier, the first time the Finals had departed from its traditional strongholds of Europe and South America (the two having previously taken turn and turn about). It was fitting, too, that supposed

underdog countries such as the two hosts, plus Senegal and the USA, should have fared so well in 2002, emphasising the spread of the game and the rising standards from these 'emerging nations'. The 2006 Finals in West Germany are to be followed by South Africa in 2010, another bold step into the unknown.

The first World Cup trophy (won in perpetuity by Brazil in 1970) bore the name of one Jules Rimet, Honorary President of FIFA between 1921 and 1954. Yet the competition itself was the brainchild of the organisation's secretary Henri Delaunay. He it was who recognised the changes professionalism had made to the face of the game and declared, in 1926, that international football did not belong under the auspices of the all-amateur Olympic Games, "since many countries can no longer be represented by their best players."

Uruguay was the first country to host the event in 1930 – rightly so, being the reigning Olympic Champions. They won a hard-fought Final against neighbours and deadly rivals Argentina though, due to the difficulties of long-distance foreign travel in a pre-jet age, just 13 nations (and only

four from Europe) took part.

The holders, indeed, failed to travel to Italy to defend the trophy four years later, and again it was the host nation that would triumph, to the delight

ABOVE Fritz Walter of West Germany with the Jules Rimet trophy after winning the FIFA World Cup Final against Hungary, 1954

when their country was denied the customary 'alternate continent' switch.) Italy retained the title against tough opposition – a record 36 nations having entered – and would, thanks to the outbreak of war, kept the trophy until 1950.

The competition at this point was played on a simple knockout basis, meaning that some nations travelled a long distance for little reward: the Dutch East Indies (later Indonesia), for instance, headed home after a 6-0 footballing lesson from Hungary. This had changed by 1950 when the Finals in Brazil were played in two league-style phases. Uruguay's 2-1 defeat of the hosts proved decisive in deciding the table-toppers, and has since been regarded as the Final even if no one official match was earmarked.

West Germany's 3-2 victory over Hungary in Switzerland in 1954 was remarkable in that the Magyars had beaten their opponents 8-3 in the group stages. No such surprise in Sweden four years later where Brazil, who'd exited to Hungary in the previous tournament in the infamous 'Battle of Berne' (three players dismissed and a dressing-room brawl), thrashed the hosts 5-2, the outstanding Pelé (still only 17) scoring

of dictator Mussolini. All four semi-finalists were European nations, and it was Europe again, in the shape of France, that would host the 1938 Finals. (Argentine fans rioted in Buenos Aires

twice. Injury in the first game of the Chile '62 Finals kept Pelé on the sidelines, but his country won nevertheless, brushing Czechoslovakia aside 3-1 in the Final.

Argentina had won the South American competitions of 1978 and 1986, the former of which they also hosted. West Germany had also made the most of home advantage against Holland in 1974, while the Spain World Cup of 1982 saw a Paolo Rossi-inspired Italy conclusively beat the Germans (who would feature in three successive Finals). It seemed, from this pattern, that countries were unlikely to win the trophy outside their own continent: indeed, that had held true from the competition's inception with the single exception of Brazil's Pelé-inspired triumph in Sweden in 1958.

England's participation in the World Cup is covered in detail elsewhere, but it is fair to say that until they provided Gary Lineker as six-goal top scorer in Mexico in 1986, they had contributed little but their 1966 win to the history of the competition. The '86 tournament would, however, go down in history for Diego Maradona's 'Hand of God' goal past Peter Shilton that sent Bobby

Robson's side home disappointed. At least they went out to the eventual winners, though beaten Finalists West Germany came back from two goals down before losing 3-2.

The success of Morocco in Mexico, beating Portugal and securing draws with England and Poland, dropped the broadest of hints that Africa would soon be knocking on the world football door. As it happened, that would have to wait until the next century, but Cameroon

ABOVE The Kashima Ibaraki Stadium in Japan during the World Cup, 2002

would prove the surprise team of the 1990 competition.

They drew first blood by defeating holders Argentina in the opening game – and though they understandably couldn't maintain that level of form, did enough to worry a Paul Gascoigne-inspired England. Argentina recovered from the shock to reach the Final, where they lost to a single West German penalty. (Having lost in the previous two, Germany probably considered it their turn.)

The grant of the World Cup Finals

to the United States in 1994 would not be without controversy. But at grass-roots level, the game was flourishing and crowds witnessed a competition that sparkled until the showcase Final itself. That Final featured an Italy managed by Arrigo Sacchi, architect of the all-conquering AC Milan side of the late 1980s. He had reversed the national team's slide to the extent that they were the pre-tournament favourites, but early defeat against Jack Charlton's Eire sounded warning bells. They did, however, make it to the Final this time.

Of the African nations, Cameroon disappointed in comparison to their 1990 performance, but Nigeria proved the rising stars this time. They headed their group with a goal difference only Brazil could better. Colombia's defeat by the host nation after an opening loss to Romania saw them eliminated. Worse was to come, however, as defender Andres Escobar, whose own goal proved decisive in the second game, was gunned down ten days after returning home.

The highest-profile casualty of the tournament itself, Argentina's Diego Maradona, was a victim of his own making. Playing in his fourth Finals (1986's 'Hand of God' goal still fresh in the memory) and fighting a battle against father time by unfair means, he failed a drug test after his country's second game and was sent home in disgrace. At least he got there: England, under Graham Taylor, had failed to qualify.

The semi-final line-up of Italy, Brazil, Sweden and Bulgaria was hardly the expected quartet – though it was the first two named giants who predictably booked their ticket to the Final itself, each by a single-goal margin. Sadly, the showpiece proved unworthy of an enter-taining tournament – a stalemate which neither side looked prepared to lose as the match wore on.

Italy's hugely influential defender Franco Baresi, who was stretchered off against Norway in the group stages and underwent a cartilage operation, made it back for the Final, and played well, but the problem was at the other end. A goalless game ended with a penalty shootout, Baggio's miss ensuring Brazil became the first country to win the World Cup for a fourth time.

France '98 was not only the final tournament of the millennium but, with 32 finalists, the biggest ever. The host nation made theirs the first new name

on the trophy for two decades, and few could say they didn't deserve their win. Manager Aime Jacquet would step down after their success, but the team he put together – with names like Barthez, Blanc, Zidane, Henry and Petit – confirmed their class by going on to win the next European Championships.

Only Nigeria of the African nations survived to grace the last 16, Holland and Croatia making it through to the semi-finals. England's participation under Glenn Hoddle (who controver-sially elected not to include Gascoigne in his squad) ended in the second round in a game against Argentina notable for Michael Owen's individual goal and David Beckham's dismissal. While third-placed Croatia supplied the top scorer in Davor Suker, it was Brazil's highly-rated hotshot, Ronaldo, who supplied the controversy at the Final itself.

A team sheet was handed in without his name on, then replaced after unspecified goings-on in the changing room. Rumours abounded, speculation suggesting he'd had a fit the night before, but his sponsors Nike had demanded he played. Whatever the truth, he failed to sparkle and Brazil could not profit from the absence of suspended French stopper Laurent Blanc as Zidane (two goals) and Petit wrapped up the coveted trophy.

The success of the 2002 competition jointly hosted in Japan and South Korea was reflected by a Final that pitched the World Cup's traditional giants, Brazil and Germany, against each other. Yet it was the spirited showings of the likes of losing semi-finalists Turkey and South Korea that would linger longer in the memory – plus, of course, Sven-Goran Eriksson's England beating Argentina and leading Brazil for a spell.

As so often, there was a shock in the opening game when former French colony Senegal put one over on their ex-masters. They passed through to the second round while France, rueing a semi-fit Zidane, went home. Germany were fortunate to beat the United States in the quarter-finals, an American equaliser wrongly disallowed, while plucky Senegal were beaten by a golden goal extra-time strike from Turkey, a country fast emerging as dark horses for the trophy. But the most memorable golden goal came from Korea's Ahn Jung-Hwan against Italy, an achievement which resulted in his Italian club employers giving him his cards!

The Final was a two-goal personal triumph for Ronaldo who put the events of Paris four years earlier firmly behind him to pick up the Golden Boot with eight goals. Germany sorely lacked the suspended Michael Ballack's

LEFT The World Cup Golden Boot Award which was presented to Ronaldo in 2002

midfield guile, while usually impeccable keeper Oliver Kahn, at fault for the opener, at least had the player of the tournament trophy as consolation.

England's display in the 2004 European Championships in Portugal was dominated by teenage striker Wayne Rooney. His two goals in consecutive games that helped bury Switzerland and Croatia went a long way to erasing memories of an opening-match defeat against France that saw the 2000 winners come back from 1-0 down to take the tie thanks to two injury-time strikes from Zidane. When 'Roonaldo' limped off with a broken bone in his right foot in the quarter-final against hosts Portugal England were again one goal up, thanks to Michael Owen. But the concession of yet another late strike brought extra time and, eventually, penalties.

England's poor record in such shoot-outs, dating from Euro 1996, continued as captain David Beckham put the first spot-kick over the bar – and, when Rooney's replacement Darius Vassell saw his shot saved, it was left to Portuguese keeper Ricardo to beat his counterpart David James and send Sven's men home with nothing to show.

The 2004 European Championships in Portugal saw the superior teamwork of Greece triumph by a single goal over the flair of the Portuguese – the first home nation to lose a Final. All eyes then turned to Germany, where the final stages of the 2006 World Cup would be held. With exactly four decades having passed since England beat what was then West Germany to secure the trophy for the first and only time, hopes and prayers were being offered for a repeat performance on the opposition's turf. Sadly, that did not happen in

BELOW Balloons are released at the start of the opening ceremony for the 15th World Cup on 17 June 1994 at Soldier Field in Chicago

RIGHT French captain
Zinedine Zidane
(left) gestures after
head butting Italian
defender Marco
Materazzi
during the World
Cup Final, 2006

the last weeks of Sven Goran Eriksson's rule – but neither did the hosts triumph.

Italy beat France in a Final that will forever be remembered for the head-butt and subsequent dismissal of French captain Zinedine Zidane in his last competitive game before retirement. The game finished in a 1-1 draw after extra time, Italy triumphing 5-3 in the shoot-out. France had overcome holders Brazil in the quarter-finals but their ageing team failed to spark, Thierry Henry in particular neglecting to live up to his club form.

England had departed in the quarter-finals, losing 3-1 to Portugal whose manager Luis Filipe Scolari had been the favourite to succeed Eriksson. In the end, deputy Steve McClaren of Middlesbrough stepped up after the Finals were over. A lack of firepower due to Michael Owen's injury, plus Eriksson's selection of rookie teenager Theo Walcott whom he lacked the belief to play, left Wayne Rooney toiling alone up front. His dismissal against Portugal was arguably due to the exhaustion and frustration that resulted.

With Germany triumphing over Portugal in the third-place Final, it was clear that once again everything had gone according to the form-book, European teams dominating in their own continent. The 2010 competition in South Africa appeared very much up

for grabs, and this proved to be the case with Spain winning the trophy for the first time with a 1-0 victory over Holland in the Final. They continued to show their prowess as the best international side in the world when they emphatically clinched the European Football Championships by trouncing Italy 4-0 in the Final in 2012.

BELOW The unveiling ceremony in South Africa of the logo for the 2010 World Cup

Chapter 8

The Future of Football

"THE FIRST PRIORITY OF EVERY-body in professional football should be to attract as many paying customers as possible, and we are kidding ourselves if we believe otherwise. Spectators are what professional football is all about. Without them it has no point, no status and no future. I know professionals who see the game as their own property and the fans as people whose part in the ritual is a kind of privilege. The positions should be reversed."

Former Football League supremo Alan Hardaker, who presided between 1957 and 1979, was hardly the most visionary of men to have held office within any of football's organising bodies over the years. He was known to be against sponsors having their names or logos on club shirts, forcing the first club to bear them (non-League Kettering) to remove them, even though for many it provides welcome and necessary income.

The League Cup, which has gone through many sponsors' names over the years, was effectively his brainchild and at times today struggles for credibility in much the same way it did when first launched in 1960. Despite this, there will be few fans who will disagree with his observations on the game's priorities. They may have been uttered in the 1960s, but they have become increasingly relevant in recent years.

Football has become big business.

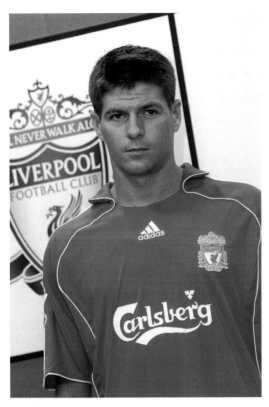

Unfortunately, however, we appear to have arrived at a situation where for many clubs 'success' is measured not in trophies or promotion won but in recording an annual profit, making dividend payments to shareholders and increasing the value of the company. When clubs are signing players based not on their individual abilities but on their ethnic origin in order to 'open up new marketing opportunities', the game's priorities are in question.

Other clubs enjoyed their own periods of success, sustained or otherwise. Arsenal emulated Spurs' Double achievement with one of their own in 1971. Liverpool repeated the feat in 1986, at a time when they were the dominant force in the domestic and European game, registering 11 League titles between 1973 and 1990

LEFT Liverpool's captain Steven Gerrard models a Liverpool home shirt sponsored by Carlsberg

Many of the clubs today are publicly quoted companies with responsibilities to shareholders, investors and the Stock Market to take into consideration.

and topping this with three FA Cups, four League Cups, four European Cups and two UEFA Cups in the same period.

Just prior to the formation of the Premier League, Manchester United began exerting their own domination, and since 1989 have been able to

parade eight League titles, four FA Cup triumphs, the European Champions League once, the European Cup Winners' Cup once and the League Cup once in front of their adoring fans at Old Trafford. Even so, Arsenal have closed the gap, winning the domestic Double twice during that period, thus proving that no domination can ever be total.

If Manchester United's achievements on the field are beyond question, their activities off it are often alarming. United probably attracted more attention for becoming the first football club in the world to realise a valuation of £1 billion than almost any of their trophy successes, the European Champions League excepted. Along with Arsenal and Liverpool, Manchester United play a prominent role in the so-called G14 group of clubs. While the richest nations in the world form themselves into G9 to decide and at times dictate world financial matters, so their footballing counterparts in G14 try to influence European football. This has seen proposals for a league involving the biggest European clubs, all of whom would presumably turn their backs on domestic football. At the same time, these clubs are behind the lobbying of FIFA and UEFA to decrease what they see as meaningless international friendlies.

As recently as 20 years ago, British players looking to earn big salaries were usually compelled to join Italian or Spanish clubs. Many top players from that era – Ian Rush, Gary Lineker and Mark Hughes – were lured away in much the same way as their predecessors Jimmy Greaves, John Charles and Gerry Hitchens were swayed by the financial rewards on offer in Italy.

The creation of the Premier League has reduced that traffic, and if anything it is now flowing in the other direction. The Football Association claimed that the 2002 World Cup Finals in Japan and South Korea featured more players who plied their trade in the FA

LEFT Ashley Cole poses with his Samsung-sponsored Chelsea shirt

THE FUTURE OF FOOTBALL

RIGHT Some of the 500 people sitting in comfort in Kensington Town Hall to watch a Wembley Cup Final on twenty TV sets, 1950

Premier League than any other League in the world, though the bulk of these were from the former East European countries and such soccer 'outposts' as Japan and China.

One of the current threats football faces is over-exposure. There will be those, most notably those who don't actually attend games, who are quite comfortable with the amount of televised football that is currently on offer. In what has become the norm, in any given week it is possible to see a Nationwide League match on a Friday evening, a Premier League match at lunchtime on Saturday, two matches on a Sunday (one of which will be pay per view), a fourth Premier League match on a Monday night and possibly three nights of European action.

The paying customer is most adversely affected by this chopping and changing of the fixture list. With unreliable public transport available on a Sunday, fans wishing to attend are forced to rely on their own cars,

thus adding to the Sunday-night traffic. Those who wish to attend midday kick-offs in the north (in the case of southern-based fans) or south (vice-versa) will often have to contemplate an overnight stay the night before a game in order to guarantee arriving at the ground fresh and on time. Similarly, those who find their clubs away on a Monday night will also incur the cost of an overnight stay and two days' holiday, all for 90 minutes of action!

The domestic cups have been said to have lost their appeal in recent years, but this seems to be one area where football, aided and abetted by the police, has shot itself in the foot. The needs of the few (ie those competing in Europe) led to the abandonment of replays in the League Cup and, if they get their way again, will also succeed in

doing so in the FA Cup. The romantic nature of the FA Cup (and to a lesser extent the League Cup) rests on the ability of a smaller club being able to force a replay at the ground of a bigger club and then complete the upset in their own backyard. Do away with replays and chances are you are doing away with upsets at the same time.

The collapse of ITV Digital in 2002 resulted in a number of clubs struggling to avoid the bankruptcy courts, usually because they'd already spent the money they believed was going to materialise

LEFT ITV Digital headquarters

BELOW The 2006 World Cup sponsorship logos

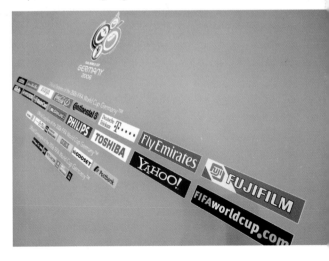

through the original TV deal. As entertaining as some Nationwide football is, it was never going to have the same kind of appeal as the Premiership. Irrespective of the moral or legal arguments that followed Carlton and Granada's decision to put ITV Digital into receivership or liquidation, the spending of money that hadn't yet been received revealed a foolhardy attitude by many clubs.

The safety and security of football's paying customers were objects of the Taylor Report, though in some cases little was done after the installation of seats where terraces once stood. But time waits for no man, and the ever-dilapidating state of Britain's football grounds, most of which were up to a century old, has led to a number of clubs attempting to redevelop their stadium or, in some cases, relocating completely.

This is good news for the spectator with sight lines, facilities, parking and comfort usually radically improved. North-east pair Middlesbrough and Sunderland had relocated to the Riverside Stadium (1995) and Stadium of Light (1997) but, unlike in Europe, groundsharing of a purpose-built new stadium was never on the agenda.

Southampton opened their Friends Provident St. Mary's Stadium in 2001, the 32,000-capacity ground double the capacity of its ageing predecessor, the Dell. Unfortunately the club was relegated in 2005, so was often only two-thirds full. As with Bolton's 28,000-seat Reebok Stadium, which opened its doors at the beginning of the 1997-98 season, naming rights were sold to a sponsor – the latest method of raising revenue.

In some cases, however, the process of building a new home has, temporarily at least, proved such a drain on resources as to endanger the financial stability of the club. Leicester City, formerly of Filbert Street, were unfortunate enough to be relegated from the Premier League at the same time as their Walkers Stadium was being

completed. Substituting Grimsby for Manchester United and Walsall for Liverpool had an unavoidable effect on attendances (as did the lack of Sky TV revenue) and the club went into administration.

Manchester City profited from the

BELOW Celtic and Japan's Shunsuke Nakamura, one of many Far Eastern players now playing for a British team

BELOW Sunderland's home, The Stadium of Light

2002 Commonwealth Games, for which the 50,000-capacity New Millennium Stadium had been built, and took up residence as tenants to the city council before the 2003-04 season. Neighbours United increased the capacity of Old Trafford to 76,000, cementing its place as the largest league ground in Britain.

Everton had aspirations to exchange the 40,000-seat Goodison Park, their home since 1892, for a new 55,000-capacity ground in the King's Dock area of the city. They abandoned their timetable to move in 2004 after the previous year's share issue had failed to yield the necessary resources. Third Division Hull had showed the way when they left their 15,160-capacity Boothferry Park in December 2002, and moved into the Kingston Communications Stadium, a new £44 million, 25,400-seat ground they share with the local Rugby League side.

Hull at least had the assistance of a supportive local council, which funded the project. Other lower-league clubs needed a rich benefactor, as with Wigan and Reading with Dave Whelan and John Madejski respectively. Athletic moved to the 25,000-seat JJB Stadium at the beginning of the 1999-2000 season, 12 months after the Royals opened the similarly sized Madejski Stadium. The club had plans to add an additional

ABOVE The Cellnet Riverside Stadium, home to Middlesbrough Football Club

5,000 seats to the East Stand if the need arose. Huddersfield's 24,000-capacity Alfred McAlpine Stadium, opened in 1994, remained one of the more impressive grounds in Divisions Two and Three.

While Arsenal had used Wembley for European matches in seasons past to test out demand, they moved into a new 60,000 all-seater stadium at Ashburton Grove (the Emirates Stadium) in time for the 2006-07 season. Ironically, many London clubs would have been more than happy to inherit their old 39,000-capacity Highbury home.

The fiasco that accompanied the planning and building of a new national stadium was symptomatic of the way the game has been run. While Birmingham and Manchester were considered and put forward convincing arguments, only London could host a World Cup Final or Olympic Games and the 'tendering' process was therefore a red herring. Wembley's redevelopment overran massively, with a delayed opening for the FA Cup Final in 2007.

But while stadiums continue to get

bigger, and audiences are growing to far flung corners of the globe, the best players of the future seem to be getting smaller – offering hope to slighter children everywhere that they too could become a Lionel Messi, at five foot seven inches tall and head and shoulders the best player in the world.

Michael Cox, who runs the website Zonal Marking, predicts: "Football will become more technical, based more around passing. For as long as the rules continue to adjust to penalise heavy tackling, it will increasingly impact on the style of football.

"Barcelona and Spain have been

talked about so much that there's bound to be some level of backlash. Because there's been such an emphasis on copying them, I wouldn't be surprised if there was a brief period of the antithesis of that, where teams become physical and maybe focus on counter-attacking more. But I think that will be a fairly short-term thing. The wider consensus will still move towards passing football.

"It's almost like a race to the bottom. If one manager is outwitted by another by being more cagey and defensive, then he has to react in the same way. I guess that's why the goals per game average over the last 60 years has generally come further and further down."

Whether the die-hard football fan wants to watch two technically brilliant teams endlessly pass the ball sideways is open to debate; many British fans still relish the blood and thunder battle where commitment and courage triumph

LEFT Andres Iniesta of Spain in action

over ability and athleticism. Maybe we haven't won anything significant since the 1966 World Cup but we still boast the most watchable league in the world!

ALSO AVAILABLE IN THE LITTLE BOOK SERIES

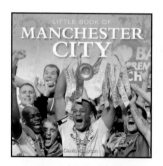

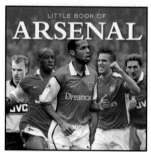

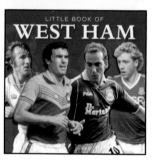